3-25-64

THE CHRISTIAN WITNESS
IN AN INDUSTRIAL SOCIETY

The
Christian Witness
in an Industrial Society

by
HORST SYMANOWSKI

Translated by George H. Kehm
Introduction by Robert B. Starbuck

THE WESTMINSTER PRESS
Philadelphia

LIBRARY OF CONGRESS CATALOG CARD No. 64-12391

PRINTED IN THE UNITED STATES OF AMERICA
PUBLISHED BY THE WESTMINSTER PRESS®
PHILADELPHIA, PENNSYLVANIA 19107

CONTENTS

PART III

THE SERVICE OF CHRISTIANS
IN THE INDUSTRIAL WORLD

PART IV

ADDRESSES FOR SOME INDUSTRIAL
CELEBRATIONS

TRANSLATOR'S PREFACE

DURING the fall of 1960, while I was studying in Basel, Switzerland, a collection of writings by Horst Symanowski appeared in German. Symanowski's name was familiar to me from discussions I had participated in concerning the effects of industrialism upon society and the need for a new understanding of the message, organization, and function of the church in an industrial society. Reading Symanowski in the light of these discussions convinced me that he had something to say to the American churches on these matters. I was confirmed in this conviction by the Detroit Industrial Mission, whose experiences corroborated Symanowski's at many points. What especially interested me, however, was the fact that he had succeeded in making relevant and fruitful applications of some key theological concepts in his ministry in the industrial world.

Three concepts particularly caught my attention. First is the concept of "fellow humanity" (*Mitmenschlichkeit*), so heavily emphasized by Karl Barth in his anthropology and in his political writings. Paul Ramsey, in his book *Christian Ethics and the Sit-In*, showed how this concept can be used in defining issues of social justice. Symanowski uses this concept in attempting to define new forms of organization and new patterns of responsibility within the industrial world which will protect a man's humanity against the dehumanizing tendencies that have shown themselves in the system of industrial work. Related to this concept of fellow humanity is the concept of the neighbor as a mode of Christ's presence in the world. This concept was heavily emphasized by Dietrich Bonhoeffer in his later period, when he was trying to understand the meaning of Christ for precisely the kind of men Symanowski found in the factories in which he worked. The "man come of age" may no longer ask Luther's question, "How can I find a gracious God?" But he still asks, "How can I find a gracious neighbor?" (see p. 50).

Here is another point at which the meaning of Christ, specifically his mode of presence in the neighbor, needs to be explored and brought into relation to the question just stated. Finally, there is the concept of the church as the community in which men, being transformed personally and corporately into the "form of Christ," learn what it means to live together as human beings. In this way, the church not only produces individuals who will function as catalyzers of new and more human forms of community in the social and political spheres outside the church, but it will itself, in the unique quality of its corporate life (*koinōnia*), provide examples of these new forms of human community. Paul Lehmann has developed a very similar concept of the church's function in society. Its relevance to economic problems can be seen in the recent book by Bruce Morgan, *Christians, the Church, and Property* (The Westminster Press, 1963. Note especially Chapter 3, "Koinonia Will Out"). All three of these concepts—fellow humanity, the neighbor as a mode of Christ's presence in the world, and the church as the community in which men learn what it means to be human—have come together in Symanowski's thought and produced an unconventional but authentic and fruitful Christian ministry at the very point in the world at which the traditional churches seem impotent and irrelevant. It is my hope that this little book may contribute to such developments in this country too.

Several of the writings published here were originally published in German. "The Church-estranged Man in the Industrial World" (1955), "The Church and Work" (1957), "Congregation Without Pulpit" (1958), "Congregation Without Walls" (1959), "An Address for the Graduation of Apprentices" (1958), and "A Sermon for an Industrial Worship Service" (1958) were translated from *"Gegen die Weltfremdheit"* (*Theologische Existenz heute*, new series, No. 79 [Munich, Chr. Kaiser Verlag, 1960]). The "Five-Year Report of the Seminar for the Church's Service in Industry" originally appeared in the *Deutsches Pfarrerblatt*, June, 1961. "Pastoral Care in Industrial Plants—Possibilities and Limits" appeared in *Die Mitarbeit*, Heft 4, April, 1959.

The translations of the following were made from manuscripts provided by Horst Symanowski himself: "Recovery or Senility?"; "Radio Address: Labor Day, 1960"; "Theses on Codetermination in the Work Process"; and "The Service of Christians to Man in the Secular World"—prepared for the World Council of Churches Commission on World Mission and Evangelism meeting in Mexico City, December, 1963. Horst Krockert, also of Gossner Haus, coauthored the latter two items.

Special thanks are due Mr. Robert B. Starbuck for the invaluable assistance he provided in the preparation of this volume. Having served under the auspices of the United Church Board for World Ministries since 1957 as a fraternal worker with the Gossner Mission in Mainz-Kastel, Berlin, and Wolfsburg, he was uniquely qualified to write the Introduction. In addition, he graciously undertook the task of reading and offering corrections of the entire manuscript. He also provided the translation of "Pastoral Care in Industrial Plants," which appears in this volume, only minor revisions having been added by me. It should be noted, too, that this article was first called to my attention by the Detroit Industrial Mission. In this and other ways their encouragement was an important factor in making this book possible.

After the translation of these writings had been completed, I discovered that at least two of them had previously been translated into English, viz., "The Church-estranged Man" and "Congregation Without Walls." The former was published in

9

the *Ecumenical Studies Series* (Vol. III, No. 3, October, 1957)
of the Council on Christian Unity, Indianapolis, Indiana. I am
not aware that an English translation of the latter was ever
published, although Mr. Starbuck tells me that it was translated for the *Kirchentag*. I had no access to either of these
translations and hence made no use of them.

George H. Kehm

Pittsburgh Theological Seminary
Pittsburgh, Pennsylvania

10

Introduction:

SERVANT WITNESSES
OF THE SERVANT LORD
by Robert B. Starbuck

I. Repentance and Renewal

What does it mean to be a Christian in today's world? More precisely, what does it mean to be a servant witness of Jesus Christ, the Servant Lord, in contemporary industrial society? And how must the church be renewed and re-formed so that it might become a faithful and credible witness to its Lord in a world that has "come of age?"

Christians all over the world are being forced to seek fresh answers to these questions. They constitute one of the most important complex of questions in the current ecumenical discussion, as indicated both by the Evanston (1954) and the New Delhi (1961) Assemblies of the World Council of Churches.

Here and there one finds places where Christians have been given the vision and the courage not only to explore these questions in their thinking but also to engage in practical experiments in new patterns of congregational life and in a new style of Christian existence in the secular world. Gossner Haus in Mainz-Kastel, West Germany, is certainly one such place, and its leader, Pastor Horst Symanowski, one such Christian.

The posing of such questions and the honest searching for answers to them are signs of that *repentance* which is the necessary condition for genuine *renewal* both in the life of the individual Christian and in the life of the church as a whole. The concrete occasion for these acts of repentance is the deep estrangement of the churches from the contemporary secular world and their consequent inability to fulfill their mission to this world.

In West Germany there are many indications of this estrangement. Perhaps the most obvious one is the fact that although 95 percent of the people nominally belong to the church, less than 5 percent (in the case of Protestants) regularly participate in the worship and life of the congregations. This estrangement is much more acute with some groups than with others. One study of 100 parishes in Westphalia,[1] for instance, indicated that whereas as high as 15 or 20 percent of people engaged in the more *traditional occupations* (such as farming, small business, clerical work, the civil service, and the crafts) go to church, in the case of *industrial workers* it is less than 1 percent. People from the more traditional callings comprise only 30 percent of those who have been baptized, but they make up 80 percent of the churchgoers and 100 percent of the church officers in the parishes studied. The estrangement is thus especially acute between the church and those groups which have been most directly and most profoundly affected by the emergence of modern industrial society.

For the overwhelming majority of West German Protestants, belonging to the church means participating in the sacrament of Baptism and in the rites of confirmation, marriage, and burial; allowing the church tax to be deducted automatically from the pay envelope; and leading a decent life as a member of a society presumably based on Christian principles. But belonging to the church has no meaning beyond this for their daily life and work in the secular world. Consequently, for them, being a Christian does not entail regular participation in the common life and worship of the community of faith. Nor does it involve any sense of a personal relationship to the living Servant Lord who calls us to share in the joy and suffering of being his servant witnesses.

12

This state of affairs holds not only for West Germany but for all the industrialized countries of northern and western Europe. Ironically, the Iron Curtain tends to divide that part of Europe where most people no longer go to church (namely, the "Christian West") from that part where a large number of people, as many as 25 to 35 percent in some cases, continue to attend church regularly (namely, the "atheist East")! Indeed, it would seem that the only modern industrial nation in the Western world where a large segment of the population participates regularly in the church is the astonishingly "churchy" U.S.A.! There are, no doubt, reasons for the "abnormal" situation of the churches here, but there are many signs that it may become much more "normal" in the not too distant future. In any case, the far higher rate of church attendance in the U.S.A. does not necessarily mean that the gospel is more relevant to the daily life and work of most church members or that it more effectively penetrates and shapes the life of society as a whole here than in Europe. Beneath the placid surface of American churchiness one senses the same profound estrangement of the church from the secular world here as in Europe.

Horst Symanowski has summed up this situation as follows: "The monstrous thing has happened: *after* Jesus Christ and *under* the proclamation of the church, God and man have been torn apart from one another."

Historians can trace the progressive deterioration of the classical medieval synthesis of Christianity and culture and the emergence of an essentially secular culture as the result of such ecclesiastical, intellectual, political, and economic developments as the split between the Western churches, the Enlightenment, the French Revolution, and the Industrial Revolution. Sociologists can analyze the progressive displacement of the church from the center to the periphery of society. Such studies can be interesting and illuminating. But they do not reach the heart of the matter. For the eye of faith, the basic cause of the estrangement of the church from the modern world lies not in the secular developments indicated above but in the failure

13

of the church to go into the "strange, new world" that they produced, as a witnessing, serving community of faith. In persisting in its conventional, traditional ways the church became irrelevant to the actual situation of men in a radically changed world. It has thereby failed to be a faithful servant witness to its Servant Lord, who came not to be served but to serve, in order that all men, in every society, might have life.

Symanowski does not condemn modern society for being secular. On the contrary, along with Dietrich Bonhoeffer, he accepts and affirms modern secular society as a world that has come of age as a result, in part, of the proclamation of the gospel. Therefore, he is not interested in disparaging industrial man for his poor churchmanship, nor in developing clever, new methods to induce him to return to the conventional, traditional church. For Symanowski, the estrangement of the church from the modern secular world constitutes first and foremost a *challenge to the church* to open itself to radical renewal through a fresh encounter with the living Word, the Servant Lord, in the midst of this secular world. It is not a matter of smuggling Christ into a world to which he is essentially foreign, nor of bringing a wayward world back to him, nor of fishing individuals out of a sea of perdition and hauling them on board a holy ship. It is, rather, a matter of opening our own eyes to his self-sacrificing, life-giving presence in the midst of *this* world, and of our becoming his faithful and obedient fellow workers. It is not a matter of "churchifying" modern man or the modern world, nor of "modernizing" the church. In the last analysis it is a question of the repentance *of the church and its renewal* for its mission as the *servant witness of the Servant Lord in the contemporary secular world.*

In the following pages I shall attempt to describe briefly how Horst Symanowski has endeavored to live out this repentance and the renewal that he and his associates have experienced. I hope that this may help American readers more fully and clearly to understand Symanowski's own writings contained in this little book.

II. THE ROAD FROM EAST PRUSSIA TO MAINZ-KASTEL

Horst Symanowski was born in 1911 in a small town in East Prussia, not an industrial region but a land of lakes and forests, Germany's former "water wonderland."[2] As a young minister during the Nazi era he played an active part in the Church Struggle and was sentenced to prison terms three times. As for many others of his generation, his participation in this struggle and his association then and since with such leaders of the Confessing Church as Martin Niemöller and Dietrich Bonhoeffer decisively influenced his understanding of the gospel, the church, and Christian existence in the secular world. Particularly significant for his later thought and work was the second article of the Theological Declaration adopted by the First Synod of the Confessing Church in Barmen in 1934:

> "As Jesus Christ is God's assurance (*Zuspruch*) of the forgiveness of *all* our sins, so in the same way and with the same seriousness he is also God's mighty claim (*Anspruch*) upon our *whole* life. Through him befalls us a joyful deliverance from the godless fetters of this world for a free, grateful service to his creatures.
>
> "We reject the false doctrine, as though there were areas of our life in which we would not belong to Jesus Christ, but to other lords—areas in which we would not need justification and sanctification through him."[3]

On the occasion of Martin Niemöller's seventieth birthday, Symanowski acknowledged his indebtedness to him in the following way: "You showed us in those days the way into the church of Jesus Christ, which does not live from the approval of the worldly or religious public, but only from the power of its Lord."[4]

Like most other members of the Confessing Church (the exceptions being those who spent the war in concentration camps) Symanowski served as a soldier in Hitler's *Wehrmacht* in both the West and the East.[5] After being badly wounded on the eastern front, he was discharged in 1943. Since he was unwilling to promise not to resume such activities as praying by name for the leaders of the Confessing Church who were serving sentences in concentration camps, and taking up offerings for the "illegal" work of the Confessing Church, he was not able to serve as a minister in the Evangelical Church of his native East Prussia. Thereupon he was offered a post with the Gossner Missionary Society in 1943, in which he has served ever since.

The Gossner Missionary Society is one of the oldest (dating from 1836) of the more than forty independent Protestant missionary societies in Germany. After it had sent missionaries to all parts of the world in its early years,[6] northeastern India became its mission field, leading to the emergence of an independent Evangelical Lutheran Gossner Church there in 1919, which is now one of the largest and liveliest churches in India. Under the leadership of its director, Hans Lokies, Gossner was deeply involved in the Church Struggle during the Nazi era. Many secret meetings of the leaders of the Confessing Church took place in its headquarters in Berlin, the doors of which remained open to Christians with Jewish background after such Christians were no longer welcome in most parishes. Since 1945, Gossner has continued to maintain close relations with its daughter church in India, but it has also been increasingly concerned with helping the church discover and carry out its missionary task in the secularized, "post-Christian" homeland of both East and West Germany.

During the flight from East Prussia to Berlin in 1945, Symanowski and his family lived for several months on a collective farm in Pomerania, where he worked as a laborer and mechanic. After giving able leadership to Gossner's innovating work in the area of training teachers of religion for the public schools in Berlin after the war (the first time a church agency had ever assumed this responsibility in Germany), Symanowski helped start its work in East Germany in 1948. In response to a call for help from a church superintendent, Symanowski and a young associate, Bruno Schottstaedt, went to the war-ravaged area along the Oder River (the boundary between East Germany and Poland) in a house trailer they had purchased from wandering gypsies. Here they found villages which had been almost totally destroyed during the fierce battles at the close of the war and which were now bulging with the expellees from the eastern provinces. Not only had the overwhelming majority of the church *buildings* been destroyed, but more important, the *congregations* had all but ceased to exist as functioning communities. The reason for this distressing state of affairs was alarmingly simple: after the pastors had been drafted and sent to the front, no one had felt authorized or equipped to engage in the "work of ministry." Therefore, in the midst of unimaginable need and suffering, the congregations had gone out of business—and this in a church that for more than four hundred years had given lip service to the doctrine of the "priesthood of all believers"! This experience made an indelible impression on Symanowski.

In this situation, Symanowski and his friend did not see it as their task to rebuild the church buildings and to seek to restore its previous order and status. Nor would this have been possible. People whom the church had for so long neglected to regard as mature fellow workers in Christ and who had had to learn to get along without the church in their hour of greatest need were not to be rewon for the church simply by drawing up new church-tax lists and restoring the old order! It was necessary for the church to go to the people where they were, to share in their life—their suffering and their labors—as fully as possible. Using their simple house trailer as their base of operations, Symanowski and his friend sought to help the people rebuild their farms and villages, in the conviction that only through such acts of solidarity could the seeds of a new church be planted in this soil. This was the beginning of what has since developed, under the able leadership of Pastor Schottstaedt, into a widespread and fruitful ministry in the midst of Communist East Germany. But that is another story.

In the winter of 1948–1949, Symanowski was asked to go to West Germany and to establish a Gossner center there, in order to develop new sources of financial support to replace that which had formerly come from the eastern provinces. Symanowski accepted this new assignment with a good deal of reluctance, preferring the "cold, clear atheist air" along the Oder to the "Christian fog" along the Rhine. Upon arriving in Mainz-Kastel, located in the midst of an industrial complex at the juncture of the Main and Rhine rivers, Symanowski found the factories bustling with activity (the "economic miracle" having begun the previous summer with the currency reform). But when he attended services in an adjacent parish with 7,000 nominal members and with a church having a seating capacity for 500 people, he found only 23 people sitting in the pews. He had not left the mission battlefield after all, but had merely moved from one front to another!

III. An Unconventional Ministry to Church-estranged "Industrial Man"

Having come hard up against the profound estrangement of the church from modern industrial society for the first time in his life, Symanowski set out to get more intimately acquainted with modern industry and with "industrial man"—his daily life and work, his anxieties and aspirations, his problems and achievements, his language and behavior. He took a job as laborer in a large cement works nearby, and for five years (1950–1954) he devoted approximately six months each year to this activity, working in a different department each year. During the summer months he devoted his energies to building a center to house what was developing into an experimental industrial ministry. For this he enlisted the support of many workers and several industrialists, as well as the help of more than 500 young people from all over the world who participated in 18 ecumenical work camps in Mainz-Kastel, most of them under the auspices of the World Council of Churches.

The completed center, Gossner Haus, has accommodations for over 100 full-time residents and facilities for a wide range of activities. From the beginning, Symanowski sought to make this center a home both for apprentices and for young industrial workers (most of them orphans, refugees, or youth from broken homes), on the one hand, and for university students, on the other, in an effort to help break down the traditionally rigid distinctions in Germany between *Akademiker* and the working classes.

Meanwhile, Symanowski was engaged in a continuing conversation with an ever-widening circle of workers, technicians, managers, and industrialists. The subject matter of these conversations was not *his* world (in the sense of "church world") but *their* world. Symanowski never sought to initiate "religious" conversations, nor did he seek to "convert" his fellow workers. He had grave reservations about both the efficacy and the legitimacy of all such methods of proclaiming the gospel to men who were deeply estranged from the church and its language and traditions. His concern was, rather, to allow the Word to become flesh in the context of areligious, worldly conversations dealing with daily life and work in the secular world.

One concrete occasion for an effort on Symanowski's part to initiate conversations with his fellow workers about the church was an invitation to give one of the major addresses at the 1955 Synod of the Evangelical Church in Germany (the federation of the 27 Lutheran, Reformed, and United regional churches of East and West Germany). The theme of this Synod was to be: "The Church and the World of Work." Symanowski believed that his should be the voice of the church-estranged industrial man, and to this end he felt he needed the help of his friends and colleagues at the factory. He therefore asked a small group of them to help him prepare his address to the Synod. Thus was born the "Friday-evening circle" which has continued to meet weekly ever since. Usually the group discusses the sermon text upon which Symanowski or one of his associates will be preaching the following Sunday, in order to help the minister with his sermon preparation. After a very brief introduction of the text by the minister, there follows a lively, earthy, and occasionally tumultuous discussion of the text, often lasting for two or three hours. Yet not one member of this group is an active church member. A few are nominal Roman Catholics, a few are outspoken atheists, most are nominal Protestants, but not one of them has the slightest interest in going to church—not even to hear "their" sermon! The language of liturgy and sermon is strange and unintelligible to them; the whole atmosphere of the traditional parish church is foreign to them. They do not feel at home there—nor do they feel that what happens there has any meaning for their daily life and work. In contrast to this, no "Bible study" on Friday evening can avoid coming to grips with the questions they pose arising out of their life—no matter how desperately some university-trained minister tries to restrict the discussion to the text in an academic manner. One high church official who once visited the group and tried to proclaim the "real" meaning of the text in an ex-cathedra manner was promptly given his comeuppance by Robert, a worker in the cement plant, as follows: "Herr Pastor, what you say may be true for your church world, but it has nothing to do with *our* world!" Karl, another member of the group, summed up the feeling of all the members when he said: "I get along very well without Sunday morning, but without Friday evening my whole week is shot!"

Not only are these workers not interested in attending church, they are also unwilling to come to Gossner Haus on Sunday. This is reserved for recreation and family life after a hectic and harried week at the factory. They are willing, however, to come together for fellowship and celebration on a broader basis than the family or a small group from time to time. Therefore, a "Gossner Sunday" is observed about every six weeks from October through April. This generally begins with a "service of worship" consisting of a free and open discussion of a text or a theme lasting for one or two hours.

Usually the service concludes with prayers in which again all are invited to participate, and usually many do, but rarely in the traditional form. The sacrament of Baptism is observed from time to time—both for infants and for adults—but never without a thorough and lively discussion of the whys and wherefores. In recent years Symanowski has finally dared to invite these church-estranged folk to participate in the sacrament of the Lord's Supper from time to time, which is celebrated around the same tables they use for the "common" meals. After the service the group remain together for the noon meal. After dinner those who have other plans for the afternoon are free to leave, but the majority usually choose to continue their "visiting" and/or morning discussion over a cup of coffee for another couple of hours. Thus in place of an hour-long service each week there has emerged a pattern of a six-hour "service" every six weeks.

About five years ago Symanowski introduced another program, which he sometimes calls "Gossner's night life." He observed that many shift workers are almost completely cut off from all forms of cultural and community life. Most such events take place in the evening between 7:30 and 10:30 P.M. Yet this is precisely the time when it is most difficult for the shift worker to get away, whether he is working the early shift (when he must get up at 4:30 A.M. in order to be on the job at 6 A.M.), the late shift (when he does not get home till around 11 P.M.), or the night shift (when he must leave for work around 9 P.M.). Symanowski learned from shift workers that the best time for them for cultural or community life was after the late shift—from 11 P.M. to 2 A.M. But there is not a very wide variety of activities taking place in most communities at those hours! So Symanowski began inviting groups of shift workers—usually from 12 to 20 men who comprised a given work group—to come to Gossner Haus after the late shift. The men are picked up at the factory gate and brought to the house. After the evening meal the group sit together around an appropriate beverage and engage in informal conversation, often until 2 or 3 A.M., after which they are taken home by members of the staff (very few German workers can afford the luxury of an automobile). During these discussions, concerns arising out of their daily work together are aired—often for the first time. The conversations touch on their relations to one another and to their superiors, their feelings about the "system," which they generally experience as a hated yoke, their hopes and anxieties, their frustrations and yearnings. It is in the context of such conversations that the Word of God must become flesh if it is to have any concrete meaning for them.

All the above illustrations show that the church cannot seek to impose its own rhythms and structures on the world it is called to serve in the name and spirit of its Lord. As a matter of fact, its own rhythms and structures are not so much the necessary expressions of its own life and message as they are reflections of the rhythms and structures of preindustrial, pre-urban society. An important element in the repentance to which also the church is called must be its willingness to give up outmoded patterns that have become a hindrance to its ministry to men in today's world. And an important element of the renewal of the church will be the development of forms of congregational life and of ministry more fitting to the life of contemporary society.

IV. Seminar for the Church's Service in Industrial Society

From the outset it was clear to Symanowski that neither the traditional understanding of the task of the church nor the traditional structures and practice of the church were adequate to meet the challenge confronting it in contemporary industrial society. He was convinced that a basic change in ministers' understanding of their task and of their relation to the laity was necessary if the church was to come to grips with this challenge. Therefore he began in 1954 an attempt to mediate some of his own experiences and insights to parish ministers by conducting month-long work camps for ministers in Mainz-Kastel. It was clear to him, however, that such programs could not begin to do the job that had to be done. What was required, as he saw it, was nothing less than a fundamental revision of German theological education.[7]

The 1955 Synod of the Evangelical Church in Germany, with its theme of "The Church and the World of Work," provided Symanowski and others with similar concerns (such as the leaders of the Evangelical Academies and the *Kirchentag* movement)[8] with a platform upon which to present their views on this problem. Among the recommendations which this Synod adopted was one concerning theological education. It urged that theological students should get acquainted with the industrial world, and raised the question whether some ministers should not receive special training for the industrial ministry at a center like the one in Mainz-Kastel. Symanowski seized this opportunity to organize the Seminar for the Church's Service in Industrial Society. The work of this seminar, which has offered six-month courses for ministers each winter since 1956–1957, is described in its Five-Year Report (see Chapter 3).

The object of this seminar is not to teach ministers clever, new methods for "reaching" industrial man, nor is it limited to training a few ministers for a specialized ministry. Its object is, rather, to initiate a basic reorientation in *all* ministers toward the mission of the church and the work of the ministry in the light of the challenge confronting the church through its radical estrangement from contemporary industrial society and in the light of a fresh encounter with the church's Servant Lord in the midst of this secular world. Symanowski is seeking to make his own modest contribution to a fundamental revision of German theological education through this seminar.

Each winter from six to twelve ministers attend the seminar. Most of them come from the various regional churches of the Evangelical Church in Germany, but there have been several from the "free churches" (which comprise only a very small minority of German Protestants) and from abroad. The majority of the participants are young ministers who have only recently completed their formal theological studies in the universities.

The majority of the alumni of the seminar are now serving in the parish ministry. It is clear to Symanowski, however, that the traditional structures and responsibilities of the parish ministry place very serious limitations on the extent to which the experiments and insights of Mainz-Kastel can be applied in the parishes as they now exist.

The average Protestant parish in an urban-industrial area in Germany has 20,000 nominal members (i.e., people who have been baptized and confirmed, and pay the church tax) and 3 ministers, so that the average urban minister is responsible for the pastoral care of about 7,000 people. Less than 350 of these people will participate with any degree of regularity in the corporate life and worship of the congregation, but the minister is responsible for administering the sacrament of Baptism and the rites of confirmation, marriage, and burial to all of them. In some parishes this means an average of almost one baptism a day, in other parishes almost one burial a day. In addition, the minister is responsible for giving religious instruction in the public schools (where this is not done by full-time teachers of religion), conducting confirmation classes, directing the various clubs and circles (most of which are totally irrelevant to the witness of Christians in the secular world)—not to mention the weekly sermon and the formidable administrative responsibilities entailed in the management of such an institution. No wonder that this whole pattern is often described as the "one-man system"!—yet the New Testament knows nothing of the concentration of all duties and functions of the *ecclesia* in one office, but speaks rather of the diversity of gifts and the varieties of service (cf. I Cor., ch. 12). Moreover, all of this leaves very little time or energy for seeking out people in the context of their daily life and work in the secular world and for exploring with them their responsibilities as servant witnesses of the Servant Lord in the myriad callings in which they are engaged.

It is necessary to supplement the parish structures with other structures more closely related to the complex, diffused patterns of a pluralistic society (the New Testament makes no totalitarian claims for the parish!) and to supplement the parish ministry with other forms of the ministry more closely related to the various callings of men in the contemporary world. About 20 percent of the alumni of the seminar are engaged in experimental ministries of this kind in half a dozen projects in various parts of West Germany. All these experiments are being carried on with the approval and support of the respective regional churches involved. In each case the basic unit is a team consisting of both laymen and two or more ministers who have been released from normal parish responsibilities in order to be free to enter more fully into the social, political, and vocational involvements of the laity in the secular world. The object of these experiments is not only the development of new patterns for the *ministry* alongside the parish ministry but also the development of new forms of witness and service for the whole *congregation.*

V. Servant Witnesses of the Servant Lord

It has become a commonplace to assert that Christians are called to bear witness to the Lordship of Jesus Christ in every realm of life. But what is the nature of *this* Lordship? And how can Christians bear witness to it *faithfully* and *credibly?*

Jesus Christ came and continues to come to us in the form of a humble *servant* (cf. Phil. 2:7; Matt. 20:28; Luke 22:27; John 13:3 ff.). His servanthood was not a denial of his Lordship, nor was the former simply a prelude to the latter—on the contrary. In the act of serving us he both exercises his sovereign Lordship over us and discloses to us the nature of *his* Lordship, which does not express itself in "lording it over" us but rather in "emptying itself" on our behalf. The Lordship of Jesus Christ is not "of this world" but of that God whose heart is *agapē,* self-sacrificing love.

Christians cannot bear witness to *this* Lordship faithfully and credibly by arrogantly proclaiming it to the world as though it were an alien yoke to which the world had to submit, much less by seeking to dominate the world in the name of this Lord. That would be to pervert *his* Lordship into the quite worldly endeavor of one institution or of one group of men to dominate others. Christians can bear witness to the Lordship of Jesus Christ in every realm of life only by humbly sharing in his servanthood in the midst of the secular world. In the words of H. D. Wendland, the church of Christ is the servant of the world.

This understanding of the inextricable interpenetration of witness and service lies at the heart of Symanowski's views on the nature of Christian existence in the secular world. These views have been most clearly and succinctly expressed in the paper "The Service of Christians to Man in the Secular World" (Chapter 7): "Precisely in relation to secular man witness to the love of God will have to take the form of service. Service is a sign of what Jesus did for the world and at the same time a report about the way he exercises his Lordship without compulsion in self-giving love."

The service of Jesus Christ to men in today's world is not limited to acts of charity toward sick, disadvantaged, and oppressed *individuals,* necessary and important as these may be. It also embraces the transformation of *institutions* that threaten man's humanity. As part of their witness to the Lordship of Jesus Christ, Christians must actively participate in every effort to modify or abolish institutional patterns that make genuine human existence difficult or impossible. The Germans have an apt word for this service: *gesellschaftliche Diakonie.*

The basis of Symanowski's *gesellschaftliche Diakonie* is his continuing dialogue with industrial man. Through this he keeps constantly in close touch with the heartbeat of the life in the factories in his area. It is constantly pointed out to him by workers and managers alike "where the shoe really pinches." Each year he selects one problem for special study and discussion in a series of five or six monthly meetings for a broad group from both labor and management. One year the theme was the impact of automation, another year the lot of shift workers, a third year trust and mistrust in industrial relations, and a fourth year the problem of peace and the economic order.

The "Theses on Codetermination in the Work Process" (Chapter 9) were the result of such a series of meetings during the winter of 1959–1960. Many conversations over a period of many years had convinced Symanowski and his associates that a far-reaching restructuring of the essentially authoritarian structure of German industrial plants was one of the most crucial problems confronting both German industry and German society as a whole. (The reasons for this are set forth in the theses themselves.) So Symanowski decided to tackle this knotty problem with even greater intensity than usual. In the course of the winter, several daylong consultations were held with a group of management leaders from the nearby factories. (One top management official from a large firm in the Ruhr felt this matter was important enough for him to make the round trip of 250 miles in order to take part in these consultations.) In addition there were numerous lengthy discussions with groups of workers and labor leaders, and with a group of theologians and social scientists. Various aspects of the problem were discussed in monthly meetings attended by 100 to 150 people from both sides of the bargaining table. Finally, at the end of the winter the theses were drawn up and then submitted to both management and labor leaders for further consideration and action. As a result of these meetings several firms have undertaken experiments as tentative first steps in the direction of developing a more democratic pattern of work in their plants.

The *gesellschaftliche Diakonie* of Christians is not a matter of working out "Christian solutions" to all the social problems confronting men in the contemporary world. Nor is it a matter of the church seeking to impose such solutions on the secular world from the outside, so to speak. Even if this were possible, it would not be *Diakonie*, but clericalism. It is, rather, a matter of lay Christians participating in the various realms of the secular world in which they are involved (such as industrial relations, race relations, international relations) in such a way as to support all movements in these realms which are struggling to overcome structures that threaten man's humanity and to develop more humane patterns of common life and work. The major responsibility of the church and of the ministry is to help lay Christians to understand that such action is an essential part of the service to which Christ calls them in today's world and an indispensable ingredient of their witness to the Lordship of Jesus Christ in every realm of life.

When Christians become deeply involved in such struggles, they soon discover that neither the Servanthood-Lordship of Jesus Christ nor the calling to be his servant witnesses in the secular world is an empty phrase or an easy lot. It always costs something and leads to conflict and suffering. Just as witness and service are inextricably interrelated in Christian existence in the secular world, so are the cross and the resurrection. As the paper on "The Service of Christians to Man in the Secular World" puts it: "The witness that Jesus Christ is risen and is the Lord of the world must confront secular men in our time in the form of sacrificial service for their sake. This happens when Christians in their work and in their social involvements reckon with the reality of the new world in the midst of the old. . . . The cross appears wherever the reality of the resurrection is seriously reckoned with among men today. They always belong together" (p. 122).

The Evangelical Churches in Germany, whether of the Lutheran or of the Reformed tradition, have always stressed the priority of the proclamation of the Word over all other tasks of the church. This preoccupation with the proclamation of the Word continues to dominate both theological discussion (whether one thinks of the Barthian, Bultmannian, or Neo-Lutheran schools of thought) and the life and work of the churches in Germany today. No one can dispute the fundamental importance of the proclamation of the Word for the mission of the church. Nor can anyone dispute the necessity of

a continual effort to clarify and deepen the church's understanding of this Word in order that the church's proclamation
of it may be faithful, intelligible, and relevant. It may be,
however, that in Germany this concentration on the *kērygma*
(the message) has taken place at the cost of giving due recognition to the nature and importance of other forms of *diakonia*
(service) in the total witness of the church. This, in turn, has
led to an overemphasis on the role of the ordained ministry
in the total mission of the church, and the failure to recognize
the crucial importance of the service of the laity outside the
walls of the institutional church. It is at precisely this point
that Symanowski has his distinctive contribution to make both
to the theological discussion and to the life of the church in
Germany today.

In this ecumenical age we have learned that each member
of the body of Christ needs to learn from the ancient traditions
and from the new insights of the other members in order to
fulfill more adequately in its own place the one mission to
which the whole body of Christ throughout the world has
been called. For this reason, this little collection of the writings
of one particular concrete situation is now being made available to the English-speaking parts of the *oikoumene.* May it
make its own modest contribution to the ongoing ecumenical
conversation and to the renewal of the church for the sake of
its mission to the world, to the glory of the living God, who is
"above all and through all and in all."

PART I. THEOLOGICAL AND SOCIOLOGICAL PERSPECTIVES

1

THE CHURCH-ESTRANGED MAN IN THE
INDUSTRIAL WORLD

THE SCOPE of my discussion will be limited to those workers who have lost any kind of binding relationship to the church. What can we do for such people? What I have to say comes out of experiences in three plants during the last three years. The plants were: (1) a chemical factory with about 4,000 workers; (2) a cement factory with about 1,400; and (3) a paper-processing plant with about 500 male and female workers. It was about five years ago that I became employed for the first time as a common laborer. Since then I have worked in the same plant during every week, month, and year, each time in a different department. Since May, 1954, the acting pastor of the parish in which this plant is located has been working four days a week as a laborer, leaving only the remaining three days free for all his church work. He has worked under this discipline for a year, in the quarry of the same plant at which I am employed. In the two other plants I mentioned, there are two Dutch men at work. The one is a full-fledged theologian, who has been there for a year and a half as a helper. The other is an "intern" of the Institute, "kerk en wereld," in Driebergen.

I. THE SEPARATION

For the church-estranged man there exists no connection between the world of his work and the church. To be sure, there is some connection between the world of his personal family life and the church, but only in those boundary situations of birth (=baptism), coming-of-age (=confirmation), marriage (=wedding service), and death (=funeral service). But these are the places in man's life that have been cultically "transfigured" by all religions. In any case, the fact that the church is resorted to in these circumstances may not be taken as proof that a real *Christian* faith on the part of the church-estranged man comes to expression here. Certainly even these people can talk about God. But he belongs to the religious realm: he has nothing to do with the everyday world, with work and with wages. Indeed, the machines run just as well without God's help. Production is the creation of man. Man is the lord in the world of work, however much God may be lord in the religious realm, in the church. One can allow himself to enter this realm on occasion, but one can also just as well leave it alone. Here is my everyday world—there is religion; here the reality of matter—there the pious ideology; here is the hard struggle through life—there an unrealistic moral doctrine; in short, here I am in my world—there is the church, outside of the reality of everyday occurrences.

The monstrous thing has happened: *after* Jesus Christ, *under* the preaching of the church, it was possible for God and man to be torn apart from one another!

II. The Incarnation

How can we make it clear to the church-estranged man that since Jesus Christ there simply is no longer any separation between God and man? Nothing at all is accomplished here by theological talk. The preaching of Jesus Christ will have to become flesh once again here and now in the world of work.

It is not enough that an interest is expressed by the church, here and there where possible, in that a "word to the social situation" is drafted, or the church-estranged man is lured to an evangelistic campaign by similar themes. The incarnation of God took place in the world. Jesus Christ didn't wait inside the Temple for those who might be interested in his message. On the contrary, he was found among those who had no access to the Temple. Thus, the task set before us is not to find a way by which the church-estranged man can once again be called into the place where Christians gather for worship. Just the opposite! In order to be followers of this Jesus we have to leave our home base and step alongside the church-estranged people, those who do not understand, irreligious as well as religious people, yes, even the godless. It is not a matter of the defense or preservation of the church but, rather, of winning men. In the Evanston Report of Section II, it was stated: "The first step in evangelization must always be not that of controversy but of identification and alongsidedness."[9] That means the renunciation of every exaggerated, nervous, hectic effort to convince the church-estranged man of the truth of our position. It is much more the very simple matter of being there with him, of standing with him in his world. It is a matter of loving the neighbor in the world of work. Let me translate thus: taking him seriously in his productivity, in his wish to improve his means of support in order to make more secure his material existence; taking him seriously in his anxiety of becoming ever more dependent upon his plant or union.

The command for such neighbor love applies to all Christians who themselves stand in the world of work. But if they are not to be found there, or if they do not fulfill this ministry there, then this task will have to be tackled by the officials of the church. And they themselves will be the first to profit if they take up this work. For there they will learn to know about those relationships which have a more enduring effect upon men today than all the church's efforts to influence those who remain outside by means of occasional missionary undertakings or public pronouncements. There they will learn about man in his normal life, his this-worldliness, and his distrust of all words designed to make a claim upon him. In living together with them, they will begin to understand how vast the area of work is in the life of those who belong to a plant, and how the remainder of their life is divided into different sectors—family, adult education, union, sports, politics, recreation, or the effort to obtain a house of their own. With astonishment they would discover that the churchly sector is either lacking or else relegated to a narrow, insignificant sector set aside for the already mentioned special religious occasions. They would see how stoutly the church-estranged man resists any expansion of the churchly sector, since such an expansion can occur only at the expense of one of the other sectors, an expense that he does not want to pay. There, at the place of work, they are at the mercy of one another day by day, for eight hours and longer. There are no possibilities of withdrawing, whether (for the church-estranged man) "to get away from this message and its bearer" or (for the churchman who has taken up the call to enter the world of work) "to move behind the pulpit, back into the circle of those who, like satisfied customers, buy the goods without complaint Sunday after Sunday," as one businessman put it. There, everything will be carefully tested, and much will be sharply contested.

I am often very uneasy when I think of how glibly we summon members of our congregations to the task of witnessing in these places, as though everything were self-evident. How harmless must this world of work seem to us when we send theological students into it to gain a little "experience"! But the world there is in fact a battleground, where not only a man's job, just wages, and daily bread are fought for, but where it is also a question of who can help save his humanity and human dignity. It is not easy to remain a Christian in this world of work. Let no one think he can turn this fallow field, so long neglected by the church, into a nice little churchly garden by means of the usual theological and Biblical tools. The land between the smokestacks of the factory is no idyllic "victory garden" of the church. There we will have questions put to us for which we have not learned any answers. We will come up against situations in which we will not know how we as Christians ought to act. We will no longer find it possible to speak so easily about proving our faith in the world.

I can well understand those theological students who come to me from the factory and declare that they no longer wish to study theology: *this* world is not to be overcome by any amount of preaching or witness. But they renounced the possibility of standing outside of this battlefield of today, to spend their lives and energy as church-employed attendants of splinter congregations isolated from this battlefield. We would have a lot more theological students today if we were able to direct them to work in the modern industrial world and were in a position to give them the necessary equipment for this work. Do you understand what it can mean to be handed over to this world? Do you understand why we cannot say so glibly, "There is the place where laymen have to prove their faith; our place is in the pulpit"? It seems to me unrealistic and unmerciful to send the few Christian workers into the battlefield where we church officials have not yet appeared or have allowed our own faith to be tested by it so little.

I would like to give you a very simple example of how little we pastors, from the experience gained in our pastoral work, know how to reckon with the laws and customs of this world of work. We are sometimes asked by church people why we want to meet the industrial worker right at his place of work instead of in his home and with his family. Once I experience with my own body the way in which the system of production lays hold of my life with inexorable laws, determining it by its own rhythm, then I understand that the worker is no longer the master of his own free time, is no longer free to shape the life of his household. His own shift work, as well as that of his wife, his older children, or other members of the family, allows no stable period of free time, no evening of rest in the old sense, and often not even a fixed day of rest each week. It is often no longer possible to speak of Sundays and holidays in which the whole family can be together. The modern system of production does not permit a man to live any longer in step with the natural rhythm of day and night, six days' work and Sabbath rest. Its work is directed neither by sun nor moon, summer nor winter. It has a rhythm of its own. Which morning prayer or which evening prayer should we teach our young men and young women who will soon be getting up in the evening and going to bed in the morning according to the demands of this rhythm? What does it mean that the time of waking and sleeping, of work and rest, are switched every eight or ten days because of the changing of the shifts? The rhythm of our churchly life in villages or in certain vocational groups may still show a harmony between the rhythm of nature and the rhythm of work, or at least it may be able to correspond to this from time to time. But for millions of men who are yoked to the modern system of production there exists *only* this other rhythm. One cannot march between two bands playing in different rhythms, however. The world of work is in fact a world in itself, which cannot be dealt with by the recipes that proved themselves in the preindustrial world.

This one little example should indicate to us, in place of many others that could be offered, the fact that it is not only the church-estranged man who is the reason for the estrangement between the church and the world. But is there any possibility at all for bringing these two worlds nearer to each other? It is certain that the church will not be able to overcome the rhythm of this other world. But the church can, out of love for those men who are yoked to this rhythm, cease making its own rhythm the precondition for the Christian and churchly life. It can attempt to participate in the life of the men who have fallen under this law. This attempt begins by stepping into this new world, and being there with them, being present with them. The British have given this task a crisp and moving description: to be—not to act.

III. THE WITNESS OF THE WORD

At this point many of you will become uneasy. Does not faith stem from preaching? Are we not a church of the *Word?* Certainly, but to be precise, we are a church of that Word which became flesh and which constantly presses toward fleshly embodiment, toward matter, toward visible shape, toward bodily existence. Speaking and being are not to be separated when it comes to following Jesus (*Nachfolge*—sometimes translated "discipleship"). And both belong together in the place of work. Speaking is a very natural and unartificial consequence of being together with people at their place of work. Please don't think of religious talk, discussions about God, in this context. We don't like to engage in this sort of thing because, for the most part, such discussions are too loose and noncommittal. It is much more a matter of factual conversation that goes to the point, and in which it is not necessary to switch suddenly to Christian and churchly matters. At Evanston, this point was put as follows: "God's conversation with his church is a conversation about the world. The church must be prepared to speak about the world if it wants to speak with God. The world is the direct object of God's activity" (D. T. Niles).

It is a widespread error, among both churchmen and men estranged from the church, that God interests himself only with religious matters. That kind of thinking is thinking in sectors. I have to guard myself against falling into such thinking at my place of work. For I have not to concern myself with the expansion of the churchly sector into another sector, but, rather, I am myself being tested as to whether I know how to speak about God only in a propagandistic way, or whether God is really the center of my life also in this world of work. This latter point can be proved only in precisely areligious conversation, however, where issues like work, pay, fellow workers and foremen, clerks and managers, the demands of the company, and the demands of the union are the substance of the discussion. In this way, the factory whistles become for us a call to the divinely ordained ministry set for us in this world. In this way we believe that we do our work and carry on our conversations inside the factory in the name of the Father, and of the Son, and of the Holy Spirit. We are of the opinion that this is already a legitimate proclamation of the Word of God.

Please think of such conversation as a very natural process. We talk about the everyday questions of job and family, the joys and burdens of life, but always very *concretely*. The Word of God wants to take shape in these worldly questions. Hardly a shift passes at the plant in which such questions are not discussed in some group. Either it is the work group or it is a group sitting together at the breakfast table. Not all forms of industrial work offer the same opportunities for such talk. But there are very few plants in which such conversations are completely ruled out. The parish workers of Burckhardthaus [equivalent of YWCA], who are engaged as female workers in Frankfurt, Offenbach, and other places, can tell you how they stand together with a great number of other women in one room, sometimes for eight hours at a stretch, and are still able, over and above the purely mechanical work to which their hands are set, to talk together or even to sing. I would like to summarize this part of my talk by referring to an essay of Professor Hammelsbeck, "The Changed World Situation of the Modern Man as a Religious Problem."[10] He says there, among other things: "Religious wrappings are outmoded as means of communication. How could a man who has been wrenched out of almost all traditions still be able to give his approval to the religious tradition? For him that will be ballast to be jettisoned as soon as possible without even trying to ascertain whether anything worthwhile was to be found in its supposed contents." We simply have to recognize the fact that the world has come of age.

Dietrich Bonhoeffer wrote from his prison cell: "I don't want . . . men in their worldliness to be made to feel like worms, but rather to confront them with God at the point where they are strongest."[11] The place where the church-estranged man is at his strongest is his place of work.

But you will ask: What happens to our responsibility to busy ourselves with the Word of the Bible? to the matter of listening directly to the text and speaking about what it says? Even that takes place in the world of work. Previously we didn't

believe that such a thing could happen. For years we were
concerned simply to understand our church-estranged fellow
workers. But now they have begun to take us seriously in our
troubles and concerns. They have noticed that Sunday preaching is difficult for us. At first they wondered ("But you fellows
have studied all that") but then they invited us to talk over
the next sermon with them. Recently we began meeting in
their houses. We bring our Bibles with us, and we have to
show them the text, which otherwise they would never find.
And then the question comes up: Must you really hold yourselves to the Bible? Really, why don't you simply leave this
sentence alone, since it is practically impossible to understand? They are a motley group. One has left the church;
another thinks that the church tax which is withheld from
his paycheck belongs under the rubric "Catholic"; a third is
interested in religion out of his pantheistic leanings; for another, the word "God" is a camouflage for all sorts of human
inadequacies. It is doubtful that any of them will ever go
into a church to hear what has become of "their" sermon.
But why should that sadden us when in fact the Word has
already gone among them and been spoken in their midst?

They will allow themselves to be invited to our house,[12]
however, in the construction of which many of them have
been helping for years. Here we hold our worship service
together with them—to be sure, not in the customary church
manner. It begins in the morning and ends in the evening—
because we remain together for the whole day, eating with
each other, discussing what is said in the morning in small
groups, as well as talking together about questions that disturb
us. It has even come to so-called "acts of the pastoral office"
("Amtshandlungen") among us, to the extent of performing
baptisms, weddings, and funerals. The question of the Lord's
Supper is still an open one among us.[13] There is not one
paragraph in the polity regulations of the church about such
forms of church life as this. But what D. T. Niles said at
Evanston applies constantly to our work: "Our faithfulness to

41

Jesus Christ places certain real limits upon our search for successful evangelistic methods; nevertheless, the love of God moves us to search for successful methods for every man."

IV. FELLOWSHIP

But it is not really at bottom a question of "methods." That is too little. To search for methods means: everything is in order in our camp; only the knack for bringing these church-estranged men into our fellowship is lacking. To be sure, it is a matter of fellowship, of bodily togetherness, of the body of Jesus Christ. Yet it is not a matter of the religious form of this body, but of its secular shape. The label "Christian" doesn't really matter. What matters is that the reconciling act of God *actually occurs in the world,* in our case, the world of industrial work. Witness to this act is not a religious but a secular social event. It leads, namely, to an alteration in the relationship between men, between fellow workers in their place of work, between them and their foremen, between employer and employee, between man and wife, parents and children. Thus does the witness to the God who loved the world and the worldly ones become salt for the earth, the preserving and transforming ferment of society. In this change of relationships between men, in finding themselves belonging to each other, the church occurs. In the Report of Section II at Evanston it was put this way: "Also, wherever Christians find themselves separated by caste, class, racial or other barriers, they will boldly cross them, manifesting Christ's solidarity with the whole of mankind. In a divided world they will fulfil Christ's ministry of peace, manifesting in their own life the new mankind which has begun in Jesus Christ." "Without the gospel the world is without sense, but without the world the gospel is without reality."[14]

This sentence cannot be taken simply as something to be carried into the modern world of work as an assertion or a demand. It can only be practiced in an unassuming way and attested in this world of work itself. Is our church today in this world? Does it stand outside of it, over against it? Who are those who are sent into this world? Who is ready to send them? Who is ready to go? And what will we say when perhaps by means of such an entry into the world of work, congregations of new Christians arise "whose form of life calls into question the normal structure of congregational life"? What will the relationship of such new congregations be to the old parish congregations? These are questions which I cannot answer and which, moreover, I do not want to answer. For such an attempt to give an answer can only mean that already today we would attempt to make a picture, to propose a program, as to how such congregations ought to look. But our wishes in this matter can easily hinder the alterations in our congregational life that God might want to create today for the sake of these men in their changed world. The Evanston Report of Section II said: "We would urge the churches to give serious thought to those questions, for they point to a challenge which the new form of society in our technical age makes to the present social structure of parish life."[15]

All this criticism should help us to perform a little better the ministry in the world of work which God has laid upon us, and which we have discussed under these four headings. We should thank God that he has given us a new start at some places, be they ever so small. Perhaps our church can take more interest in these attempts than it has heretofore, and even share some of their burdens. The Christians must recognize more than they have up till now that God does not simply call the church-estranged man to the places where our parish congregations are located, but that today he wants to go with us to the many in order to win some of them and with them to build a congregation that ministers to the world. This may mean for the church an exodus out of its familiar and intimate land. But what Christ said must also be valid for the church: "Whoever would save his life will lose it, and whoever loses his life for my sake will find it."

2

THE CHURCH AND WORK

NOTHING new about this theme, you may be thinking. The Bible already had lots to say about work long before the theme we think so modern, the "world of work," came into vogue. Yet I think the character of work has changed radically, so that work today is no longer comparable to the work the Bible spoke of.

I

Permit me to name a few of the distinguishing features of work today that one could not find in the work of preindustrial ages.

1. We no longer work directly for other men, as was once the case with, e.g., tailor and shoemaker, and still is the case for those in the so-called "service professions." Under the present system of production we work for things and on things, often without any idea what the products of our work will be used for. That is to say, man has dropped out of our vision of our work. We work *with* men, to be sure, to an even greater extent than in previous ages. But we no longer work *for* men whom we know.

2. We no longer work in family groups, as perhaps the farmer, butcher, or storekeeper still does today. Rather, we work separated from our families, the wife perhaps working

at a place different from that of her husband, and a child at still another place. How many wives have never become acquainted with their husband's place of work and vice versa? They can't help each other at all in their respective callings, unless one considers the pay envelope sufficient help in this regard. At the marriage altar the pastor still says the beautiful old words about the woman being made as man's helper —and, indeed, he means *this* woman of *this* man now before him. But doesn't the pastor know that after the honeymoon this man will work days on end with other girls and women, and that this woman will work with entirely different men? What should he say to them at their wedding in view of this situation? It is astonishing that so many marriages still endure despite these circumstances. To be sure, our films are full of themes like "the boss and the secretary" because the threat against marriage that exists in situations where husband and wife no longer work together has been perceived. But we should also recognize that a lot more love and a good deal more strength is needed in married life today than was needed in times when the wife brought a few acres of land and a few cows with her into the marriage, thus setting up a "partnership" that could not thereafter be dissolved. We should be very thankful for the many good marriages that do exist today.

3. Work is no longer a matter of "daily work" but of "shift work," consisting of so and so many hours. It is a matter of indifference whether these hours fall at night or during the day. Whether we like it or not, we have to let night be day and day be night. What is written in Psalm 104 and many other places is true for the lion and his brood, but not for man: "Thou hast made the darkness, that it may be night, in which all the wild animals prowl, the young lions who roar after their prey and seek their nourishment from God. But when the sun rises, they cease from this and lie down in their dens. Then man goes forth to his work and tills the ground until evening." Does it really mean nothing at all

45

that man has abandoned this rhythm in the industrial enterprise? The "night life" of our big cities leaves a bad taste in the mouths of many churchgoers. Why isn't it the same for the "night work" of thousands of men?

4. Machines require no rest at night. They don't need the yearly rhythm of nature. Thus, it is a matter of indifference to them whether the sun is shining or whether it is raining or snowing or freezing outside. But along with the machines, man too has become independent of these natural factors. We can keep the temperature of the workshops constant by means of air conditioning. The year is divided for us at only one point: our vacation. At this time we even begin to take an interest in the weather. Here the sun and the rain really do affect us. This is really our time of rest, and in it we even participate in the rhythm of nature once again in our waking and sleeping life. This is the great Sunday of the year for us.

5. In our industrial society we have often lost Sunday as the seventh day of the week (by Jewish reckoning) or as the first day (by Christian calculation). One thinks, in this connection, not only of the men who work in continually operating plants or those whose workweek is constantly shifting, but, above all, of the millions of men in the so-called "service professions." The traffic keeps on rolling even on Sundays; hotels are filled to overflowing; patients have to be cared for in the hospitals; doctors, druggists, firemen, and laborers have to be ready to serve; and the police are continually on the go. Is Sunday still a day of rest, not to speak of a "day of celebration" (*Feiertag*)? Does anyone still think he can turn back the wheel of progress on this development?

6. The rhythm of machine work has changed us all, not only those who work at these incessantly moving machines. We have become men whose time is chopped up and divided into ever smaller units: the day into three shifts, the shift into eight hours, the hour into minutes and seconds, in which I have to operate according to the plan of the timekeeper or

the stopwatch behind me or the timetable in my pocket. We live in moments. What was yesterday? Who can still plan for the future? We do not seem to be able to anticipate, while it is still fall, that we will soon need a winter coat. So we wait until the moment comes when it is cold before we buy one. My factory sees to it that I get a supply of coal and potatoes in my cellar and pay for it in installments. We do everything in installments because we have no view of the whole. Everything has fallen apart into smaller units. It is for this reason that Bonhoeffer could say that modern man is in the clutches of a deep forgetfulness: he has no access to his past anymore, and he can meet the future with only a playful attitude. It is a fact: who can still remember which film or which TV program he saw last week? Yes, and who still knows what happened among us in the last twenty-five years? Have we really overcome this past, or have we merely covered it up with the complaint, "Oh, don't stir that up again"? Don't we in fact take a playful attitude toward the future? If this were not so, the topics of conversation in our plants after each Thursday and up till the next Wednesday would not be "lotto" and "toto."[16] We meet the future with a game!

7. The consequences of such a splintered and breathless mode of life are felt in the most intimate sphere of our lives, in the family. Even the two landmarks of our life, birth and death, have already been taken out of the context of the family. How many people today are born at home, so that older children of the family experience the peculiar atmosphere of a birth, which makes life and death seem so closely related as to be almost brother and sister? Nowadays people are usually born in the hospital in room X on the first floor, while deaths occur in room Y on another floor. Do most of us realize that we do not even know what a birth room or a death room looks like, although in earlier days (and perhaps still in the country) this was common knowledge? Why do we really wonder that today people no longer seek pleasure in their family, but prefer instead some anonymous place for

their amusement, which is offered to them by an often spiritually empty and intellectually inferior but business-wise entertainment and film industry?

II

These are only seven signs of the altered situation that prevails in the world of industrial work. There are others, and everyone may add things that he is familiar with, and which threaten him in particular. But now we have to see that this changed world has also changed man's relation to religion in general, and, in our case, to the church in particular.

1. The man of the industrial age knows himself to be liberated and independent at a specific point in his life. This became very clear to me several years ago when I was in India. I saw the peasants in the villages, who today comprise about 98 percent of the population of India, filled with anxiety about the harvest—whether it would be large enough to carry them through the year and allow them to have enough left over to carry them into the next year. Again and again they are faced with hunger, and hundreds of thousands of them die of starvation annually. For this reason, everything depends upon rain at the right moment and in the right quantity. If the rain is late, adherents of the primitive religions begin to tear at themselves until blood runs, in order to call upon the rain gods. The refined Hindu priest sacrifices hens and goats that people bring to him, to induce rain. And the Christian congregations gather for prayer services in order to implore heaven for rain.

In the middle of the jungle, however, I learned of a congregation in whose midst a very modern cement factory had been built three years earlier. As I inspected this plant, accompanied by twelve Christians who worked among the thousand other workers employed there, I saw something I had never found anywhere among the village dwellers. These industrial people held their heads high. They knew that they were no longer dependent upon rain and sun as their relatives outside of the factory were. They didn't work for only three months and then become inactive until a new rainy season arrived, as those who worked in the fields did. Rather, they earned their daily rice twelve months of the year. They knew what factors were necessary in order for their plant to produce and thereby provide them with the necessities of life: (a) raw material in sufficient quantity for several centuries could be found in the vicinity; (b) machines and spare parts, for which the engineers were responsible; (c) energy, in other words, coal, for which the production managers were responsible, and which sometimes had to be imported from distant places just as we do here; (d) a work force, men, in sufficient quantity were available; and these needed daily rice just as much as the machines needed the power supply. Rice had to be imported in cases of an insufficient local supply. Now, upon whom is this man in the industrial world dependent? Upon rain? Upon the harvest in the vicinity in which he lives? He can no longer understand why the "animalist" tears himself, why the Hindu priest offers animal sacrifices, or even why the Christian congregations hold prayer services. In his existence as an industrial man he is no longer in the same condition of dependency as the others who still live in the old peasant society.

This is precisely the same development that we have passed through in Europe, except that it has occurred in one generation in the instance just cited. Its end product is a man for whom the cornucopias and squashes on the Thanksgiving altar are no longer signs for the preserving grace of the Creator. "Before the monetary reform, your God sent us rain and we hungered," say my co-workers. They are more ready to give thanks these days if I talk to them about the plants having been able to continue production throughout the last year because the world market was stable and this because the cold war didn't become hot. All of this means: in industrial society, man has become independent. He has achieved adulthood (*ist mündig geworden*) at those points in his life in which earlier generations showed themselves to be dependent and immature.

2. But there is another place at which the dependency and immaturity of industrial man is so evident that no one today will deny it. Man, today, has become dependent as never before upon other men. We all know this when there is a strike, say, in the transportation industry or in the mines or in some other branch of industry. We know how small our earth has become, and that even people on the other side of this little earth ball will not remain unaffected by what happens here, and vice versa. So man's dependency has become transposed: he no longer feels himself threatened by some high being or by nature, but by other men. The question of previous ages, such as, e.g., Luther's question when he was in, and even after he had left, the monastery: "How can I find a gracious God?"—this was the question that drove men, was the motor of their behavior in the world, unleashed crusades and started wars. It drove man and wouldn't let him sleep. But how many people today are awakened to rise and seek an answer to this question? Most of us sleep on it pretty well. Either we don't ask it, or it appears to us as a mere historical, antiquated question. But another question does drive us around, unsettles us, agitates whole peoples, and forces us into anxiety and despair: "How can I find a gracious neighbor?" How can we still live together? Man and wife, superiors and subordinates, colleagues in competitive struggle, and finally, one people with another, East and West? Here we become excited, ask questions, and seek ways. The question of a gracious neighbor has become the cardinal question of our industrial society. Who has the answer? Communism with its ideal society? Or the West with its idea of the free personality? Or, as a mediating possibility, a modified and revitalized socialism?

3. Each of them, as well as the other ideologies, will have their own partial answer to give. And there will be some partial truth in all these answers. But the fundamental answer

50

has long since been given, unappreciated and misunderstood, shut up inside the church and only seldom lived in the world. God himself gave the answer when he came near to us, so near as to become our neighbor, in the man Jesus of Nazareth, Jesus Christ. Without considering that men had no desire for this neighbor—"he came unto his own and his own received him not"—he nevertheless remained with men. Yes, even the place where they believed they had gotten rid of him for good, namely, the gallows erected for him, he made into a seam, a welded joint, so that a separation between God and the world, heaven and earth, spirit and matter, was no longer possible. He stays close to us and is our neighbor no matter where and whom we may be. Following him, being a Christian, can therefore only mean being with him close to other men, becoming their neighbor. That is the way we have to fulfill today the answer God gave to us in Jesus Christ: to become neighbors. Since this Jesus of Nazareth moved upon the earth as *the* Christ, God is in the midst of men; he doesn't have to be tediously sought in some "beyond," or hunted out of some "transcendence." He is among us! He doesn't will to be sought by some hand-over-hand climb in a vertical direction, but, rather, he moves among us on the horizontal plane.

III

This point has some consequences for our church. These will be indicated here in a cursory way. We are not in a position to paint a completed picture of this church. In fact, that is prohibited by the commandment against making graven images or likenesses. We will content ourselves with the use of only one picture which the New Testament congregation used, and which is in fact more than a picture, viz., the *body* of Jesus Christ.

1. A body is an organism, not an organization. In an organism it is a matter of the functional capabilities of all the members. The whole suffers when a part fails to function. A

51

bodily member that no longer functions properly lames the entire body, and burdens the other members. Is there any reason to suppose that things are different in the body of Jesus Christ? In every factory today cooperation is important. Only by means of a harmonious interplay of different functions (e.g., directing and executing, planning, producing, and selling) can success be attained. For this reason the factory is an organization. A congregation is more: it is an organism whose head and heart is Jesus Christ. But we are the members. Do we dangle like lame hands from this body? Are we blind eyes? dumb mouths? deaf ears? Everyone has to ask himself these questions when he sees himself in his congregation or at his place of work. We have to measure every congregation by this standard, and our Evangelical Church in Germany, and even the whole of Christendom spread across the earth. How do things stand with our functioning?

2. For example, what about the functional ability of our tongues? The tongue is "a little member which causes great things" [James 3:5—Luther's translation]. But who in our congregations makes use of this important member? If speaking is really such a significant thing, it would be very important for our congregations to learn how to do this. We ought to be ready "to give an answer to every man concerning the ground of the hope that is within us" (I Peter 3:15). A child never learns to speak without first stammering. But where is one allowed to do this in our congregations? The usual run of talk is pompous and has to be theologically impeccable.

If anyone actually does stand up and utters an opinion that seems less than 100 percent correct, there is always a theologian to get up quickly and straighten him out. Deviations to the right or to the left are not at all relished, but are annoying not only in the structures of authoritarian states but also in the church. For this reason, the pastors are the ones who do most of the talking in our congregations. Afterward the "laity" is supposed to go out and shout from the rooftops, that is, in their offices and factories, organizations and unions, what they have heard in church. But how are they supposed to be able to do that if they have never had any practice at this? The congregation is the training field in which we must learn how to speak properly. I'm not thinking about rhetoric in this connection, but of finding the right word for the concrete situation. Therefore, the everyday matters in which we are involved in the family and at our place of work, in politics and in unions, in the sports arena and in the movies, belong in the conversation of the members of the congregation. Here is where they must practice what they are to answer tomorrow. The front line exists, not between the pulpit and the pews, but between the gathered congregation and its work in its "dispersion" in places of work and in daily life. We saw that we are called to follow Christ, and to become neighbors for our fellowmen. That is what we have to practice on the drill field of our congregation (the congregation is more than this, but can you suggest a better comparison?).

There are congregations who have recognized their work and who drill together in view of it. There are different ways in which this may be done. The pastor can prepare his sermons together with other men, and where possible bring in those who exist either on the periphery of the church or outside it altogether. In Mainz-Kastel, at the Gossner Mission, the whole work of preparing the Sunday sermon is carried out on Friday evenings among men and women who for the most part have lost or have only the slightest contact with their churches, but who still see and practice their responsibility in their calling. It is impossible to tell who learns the most here: the pastor for his sermon, or his friends for the mastery of their daily existence as workers and employees.

3. We should be ready to give an answer, we hear from The First Letter of Peter. Thus, we are supposed to answer. But are we questioned at all? Perhaps we can compare the church to a radio station that keeps on transmitting on a

wavelength for which there are no longer any receiving sets, without being moved in the slightest by this fact. That is a serious question. For this reason, we have to keep our mouths shut at first, and simply listen. Perhaps the men have no "religious" questions, but, rather, entirely everyday questions. We have to take just as much interest in the nonreligious questions, because we are to be neighbors to all men. We have to love them not because they are so lovable but because God has made them the objects of his love no less than he has done with us. Yes, indeed, God loves the worldly, the nonreligious, asocial, amoral, extraecclesiastical people of all kinds. Can we do the same? "To love" is a great word and a great matter. Let's shrink it a bit and call it merely the task of taking the others more seriously, or at least as seriously as we take ourselves. If we did that, we would soon see what he cannot appropriate as part of his own existence, and what reasons he has for refusing. Our task would not be to drag him into the church in one way or another, but, rather, to go the second mile with him if he asks us to accompany him on the first. His thought and not my own would become important. His problems would keep me busy. We would share his despondency and his hopes. This is what Paul means in Rom., ch. 12. But I must also reckon with the fact that something new happens to the two of us on this common way: a Third enters and makes of our encounter and our way a piece of congregation in which this Third party is listened to and in whose name the right word is found.

4. It is a matter of speaking, of the "word." But this is not to be separated from what in the New Testament is called *martyria*, "*witness.*" Not only the mouth but the whole body is needed for witness. For this reason, preaching alone is not yet witness to Jesus Christ. The members of the body are not like so many puppets moved by someone else. They stand in direct connection with the head of the body, in this case, with Jesus Christ. They do not move in isolation from each other, but, rather, they move toward one goal and pur-

pose, namely, that God may draw near to men in the midst of our world of machines. Where this happens, a congregation springs up and the church is established. It may not look like the appearance of the church we have grown accustomed to. Its worship will have an entirely different style, perhaps not even taking place on Sunday morning. Perhaps it will no longer have only one person doing the talking, but will allow anyone to speak who has reached maturity. The celebration of the common meal will perhaps be a little less festive, but nevertheless it will be restored to the status of an important constituent of their fellowship together, something that draws them quite close to each other in common eating and drinking, as it was for the early Christians. Traditional forms will be broken, confessional boundaries antiquated. But the congregation will be like a city set on a mountain, which will be like a light shining in our world, even our world of work.

5. In conclusion, the old question: What should we do? We ought to follow the Lord Jesus Christ. Whence? On his way to men, to all men. How does this happen? By seeking other men, moving close to them. But let's have no illusions about this: this is a dangerous business! It has nothing at all to do with a little friendliness, or backslapping (if that is possible). Being a neighbor cost Jesus his life. Will we get off any cheaper? At any rate we will not be able to count on a "meritorious cross" or anything of the kind by taking this way. Just as God made the cross the beginning of a new life and a new world and a new people, we can also count on something new being given to us today on this way toward our fellowmen. This is not a way out of the church, as some people may think, but a way into the church of God. Nor is it a matter of pulling people back and organizing them into the church, but only of moving forward and counting on God to build up his church anew in the midst of this world of work and with the men of our time. Its distinguishing features will no longer be steeples and bells, things that

have already been overshadowed by apartment houses and drowned out by factory whistles. But God can take the mutual conversation of these men, their concern for each other, their common eating and drinking, and many other things, and make them into signs that will show that they are members of one body. It is not a matter of revitalizing a sleepy and apparently dead church, but of God's new creation in the world. Our task is not to produce people to fill in the empty pews in our churches. Paul was uncompromising when Peter attempted to turn heathens first into Jews before allowing them to become Christians. Today he would oppose just as strongly the attempt first to change the men of our time into men like those who sit in our churches, getting them to accept their concepts and forms of life. Even today becoming a Christian is not a matter of circumcision, but baptism! This means: we can reckon on the possibility that in the midst of darkness light may appear; that those who are far from God may find God very near; that the Kingdom of God lies not in any "beyond," but exists and grows in our society. Then our theme will no longer be: The church *and* the world of work. Rather, it must be: *The church in the world of work.*

3

FIVE-YEAR REPORT OF THE SEMINAR FOR THE CHURCH'S SERVICE IN INDUSTRIAL SOCIETY

To DATE, five half-year courses of the Seminar for the Church's Service in Industry have been conducted at Gossner Haus in Mainz-Kastel on the Rhine. Ten regional churches from East and West Germany have sent pastors and vicars to these courses. In addition, young theologians from the U.S.A., England, Finland, Iceland, Holland, and Austria have taken part. The following is an introductory account of this half decade of seminar work.[17]

I. THE PLAN OF STUDY

Each of the half-year courses began on November 1 and moved through three phases.

First Phase: Lectures on economics, the industrial plant, social history, sociology, socialism, Marxism, the history of the political parties and labor unions, inspection of plants, discussions with management and members of the workers councils.

The instructors came from universities, technical colleges, institutes of economics and social studies, as well as from the headquarters of labor and management groups in the heavily industrialized area of the Rhine-Main juncture (Mainz-Wiesbaden-Frankfurt-Darmstadt- and Mannheim-Ludwigshafen).

Second Phase: Eight weeks of work either on the production line or in the offices of one of the surrounding plants. Working as normal workers with lengthened weekends, as shift workers with night work and Sunday work, as commuters with a trip of several hours back and forth from the plant, or as an office worker, the theologian learns the rhythm of work and the existential problems of men in the present-day industrial enterprise.

During these two months the members of the seminar were to test the analyses and assertions they had heard during the first phase about man in the industrial world. They were also to determine for themselves the extent to which the settled patterns of life and thought in their own theological existence withstood the actualities of the industrial age, and to what extent things like their prayers, Bible-reading, thoughts about themselves and others, about the church and the world, about Christian and non-Christian existence, the usual pattern of their relations to their fellowmen as individuals or in groups, the pattern of their leisure and Sunday activities, and many other things could persist in this situation. They were to ask themselves how the Christian faith and the preaching of the gospel of Jesus Christ could achieve significance for men whose thinking and living is stamped by these conditions. In order to accomplish this, a certain critical distance from a man's own calling to the pastorate is needed, whether he has already been engaged in it or is still preparing for it. The same sort of distance is needed from the routine images and unquestioned aspects of church life. The participants learn to look at the church "from the outside," through the eyes of their fellow workers. One can ask himself: "What do you as a worker think of yourself as a pastor? What do you think about the church when you view it from your position among the machines?"[18]

Third Phase: Discussions about the *consequences* of all this for the witness of the church in contemporary society, and for theological thought and theological education. This was the most difficult phase in all of our course, because it became evident very quickly in this phase that the theologian was badly overmatched. "Is it not a sign of terrifying helplessness that we have a theology which in its historical and systematic aspects has been developed and articulated in great detail but which does not for a moment possess the necessary categories for grasping the social reality of the life and work of countless millions?"[19] Heinz-Dietrich Wendland's assertion expresses exactly the feeling of the members of the seminar after the first two phases of the course. A new task of painstaking, consistently pursued theological work becomes visible here, the mastery of which can only be begun in the last phase of the seminar. Our procedure consists essentially in surveying the thought of contemporary theologians to see what they have to offer for opening up new paths for the witness of the Christian church in present-day society and for Christian existence in the world. This work must now be continued among circles of seminar alumni that have developed in various regional churches, and also from among those who have been stimulated by them through local pastors' conferences, seminars, Academies, and other gatherings. Every year alumni of the seminar meet together in Mainz-Kastel for a week to present to one another and to learn from one another the results of their further theological and practical work and thereby extend the discussion begun during the third phase of their six-month courses. The great majority of former seminar participants want to maintain this contact, which the seminar solicits by means of newsletters.

II. INDUSTRIAL PRACTICUM FOR STUDENTS

Meanwhile, the necessity arose for establishing an industrial practicum for theological students in addition to the half-year courses designed exclusively for pastors and vicars. This practicum takes place each year during the students' vacation months, from August to October. Work in industrial plants stands in the forefront of this program. The practicum is divided into three days of general orientation, eight weeks of production work, and three days of concluding discussions. Because of the financial needs of the students, the amount of time spent at work cannot be shortened in favor of the theoretical part of the program. The participants do gather twice a week, however, to discuss either a lecture that has been recommended to them, or the problems of their working environment.

The intention of the practicum is to confront the young theological student with the reality of industrial society while he is in the midst of his theological studies so that he may incorporate into his study his knowledge of life in this society, and to make clear to him that theological witness to the hope and future of mankind must be a witness that speaks to *these* men. "Without the Church, society knows nothing of the true goal and future of man. On the other hand, only through confrontation with society and through the search for man in his social reality can the Church recognize where and how it can and must carry out its service today."[20]

III. INDUSTRY AND SOCIETY

The *name* of the "Seminar for the Church's Service in Industry" is, as we have come to see, problematical. "Industry" is not the whole of society. It is not the whole of life for an individual. Thus it is understandable that some regional churches have adopted a skeptical attitude to the invitation of the seminar, arguing, in their words, that they do not desire any "specialization" for their pastors because they want to avoid "fragmentation" of their theological development into a variety of narrow concerns. Thus, the name of the seminar led to an overly narrow understanding of its purpose, as though it were designed to equip men for "industrial evangelism" or to be "worker pastors." This was not at all what we had in mind when the seminar was founded. In reality, it was the question of our present-day society as a whole that provided the impulse for the seminar. We were concerned with the whole social realm in which the life of men is rooted today, in which we all live, and into which the Christian congregation as a whole must understand itself to be sent to bear witness.

Perhaps the seminar ought rather to be called Seminar for the Church's Service in Industrial Society. [This is, in fact, the present name of the seminar—Translator.] Yet that too would be a makeshift solution because "the proper name for this our age has not yet been found."[21] The seminar does use the commonly accepted concept of "industrial society," however, since it does express an insight that we cannot bypass: that the essential characteristic of this society is the transformation of man's *work*;[22] thus, "the fact that we have to deal today with one single massive process of industrialization, which is gradually and in diverse forms of manifestation laying hold of the whole world."[23] The effects of this process have by no means been limited to alteration of the life of the worker.[24] Far beyond that, it has given birth to a new kind of society such as never existed before in the history of mankind. It has changed the forms of work and the relation between life and work in wide areas outside the industrial plant—in the "agricultural industry," as well as in handicrafts and trade, administration and offices—from the most intimate sphere of family life to the broad sphere of international life. We have lost our orientation in this process of rapid transformation, and therefore we have lost, as Paul Tillich puts it, "the courage to be." To orient ourselves by images of past forms of society is romanticism.[25] The seminar quickly shatters ready-made cliché images of the structure of human society, including uncritically accepted models of family and vocational life, individual and community, authority and subordination, property and rights of disposal, institutions and organizations.

IV. Society and Church

As these customary conceptions become questionable, the seminar members, in many cases, find themselves in a crisis. They ask: Why were we not made aware sooner of this radical transformation that has overtaken the individual man and the whole society? Why must our studies, especially our introduction into theological thought, of all things, be conducted in isolation from knowledge of this transformation?

This is indeed an important problem. The office of the theologian—and the preparation for it—is founded upon a double requirement, which is usually only half recognized and half fulfilled. On the one hand, he must resolutely and undisconcertedly turn away from the conditions in the immediate world in which he is living and from the appeals and imperatives of the present. He must turn "back" to the history of the Biblical Jesus. In the exclusivity of this orientation—in the *solus Christus* of the Reformation!—lies his Christian freedom from the world from which real freedom *for* the world can then emerge. On the other hand, the gospel is directed toward "the congregation which is at the same time oriented toward openness, and toward society. . . . The congregation obviously sees itself thereby permitted to go out beyond itself, to break out of its own realm of life, and to participate in a movement that transcends ecclesiastical bounds."[26] This means, however, that that theologian must now, no less resolutely and undisconcertedly than before, turn himself toward the present situation of the congregation, which should be a community of witnesses in this society. This turning is also a theological act, essential to the fulfillment of the office of a theologian!

In every one of our seminar courses, consciousness of the first part of this double requirement was obviously deeply ingrained into the members. They all understood that it is unconditionally necessary for theological study to be continually aware of its relation to the original apostolic witness, the historical origin of the church and its faith, and that it transmit the "techniques" of this backward reference, exegesis, and systematic theology. This other turning, however—the turn toward the concrete social environment—this is lacking even among pastors who have worked for years in a particular place and in a specific environment! Often their conceptions of family and work are still patriarchal; they speak and think about work and vocation as if we still lived in an agricultural and handicraft society. When it comes to the problem of understanding the political order, they still use a few handy concepts from an earlier metaphysical conception of the state, continually handing out the ideas of governing authority and subordination as if we still lived in the religiously based order that determined the ethos of our fathers.[27]

The responsibility for such an unfruitful conservatism in social orientation is not to be placed upon the pastors alone, however. The congregations that "want their pastors to be this way," and who determine the image of the pastorate much more than the theologian himself (which, again, is connected with the social composition of the congregations), also have to be asked where they see the basis for their existence and their task. The members of the seminar recognize this, and they write, looking back upon their six months of concentrated experience in the modern industrial world: "The industrial society demands not new methods of ecclesiastical activity, but a new form of existence for the congregation in the world. The ideal, revived during the Church Struggle, of the 'core congregation,' which acts outside itself but nevertheless keeps itself at a distance from the world, is obsolete. What was right yesterday is false today. Static thinking in terms of two realms, here the church, there the world, is unbiblical. The congregation emerges only in the confrontation of the gospel with the world."[28]

V. Church and World

But where does such "confrontation of the gospel with the world" occur? In the Sunday sermons of pastors? In special evangelistic efforts by preachers and evangelists? In the everyday existence of Christians?

If we realize that the "world" is not a conglomerate of human beings, a mass of individuals with their thoughts and deeds, but, rather, a complex, *structured* society,[29] then we must ask how man encounters the gospel precisely in this structured society. (We are of the opinion that there is no such thing as "man" or "man as such" *apart from* this social context.) *In* this society: that means in the structures, institutions, and groups in which men have learned to organize new relations from "I" to "we" in this new age. These things lie, for the most part, outside the purview of theology and the church. They cling anxiously to "natural orders," which they say have been violated or subjected to distortion. They regard with distrust or hostility the "artificially" constructed forms of organization in society, with their characteristic openness and anonymity, their voluntary associations and interest groupings, their governmental apparatus and media of communication. Dietrich von Oppen, in the book we have frequently cited here, has performed the service of showing that the despised, organized forms of human relationships are not neutral territory for the gospel! The "organization" of human relationships—and this is a prevalent fixture of our society—awaits fulfillment by the gospel! In modern society "there has reappeared the simultaneous critical and foundational relation which . . . the gospel possesses with respect to all historical forms of life."[30] We must succeed in interesting the men who live and bear responsibility in the various organized social groups. The encounter between the gospel and the world which the Christian community is commissioned to bring about will happen in this way. Otherwise, theology will remain in dialogue with itself, and the result will be simply monologues by theologians in the presence of a congregation gathered under a pulpit. The extent to which the churches have subsided into such introversion is very keenly felt by the men who bear heavy responsibility in their social groups and who are constantly and consciously involved with men outside the church.[31]

Our seminar brings the participants together with such men every semester, and in many conversations the view of Heinz-Dietrich Wendland is substantiated: "that they have much more to ask than contemporary theology and preachers can answer."[32]

It is a fact: we do not have the answer for many questions. But it is of decisive importance that we theologians learn to *hear* the questions men in our society are asking, and that we learn to assume coresponsibility for thinking these questions through with just these men. This is what we try to do in our seminar. Space permits us to sketch only a few of these questions here.

What is the meaning of personal worth and responsibility of man before God for the ordering and organization of *work* in an industrial age? What does this mean for the forms of authority and subordination, for the power to give orders and the status of receiving orders that have been developed in this age? What is the meaning of the change that has occurred in the nature of property, from being a means of providing the necessities of life to an individual owner, to a concentrated production and power factor in society? What is the significance of this change for the social class structure and for the individual man in our time? What does a man need, to come to terms with the diverse demands made upon him by the different and often competing areas of his life? What responsibility do individuals and social and political groups have today for peace, and what is the responsibility of the Christian community with respect to this and all the other questions? What does the church's Christian faith and witness to Jesus Christ have to contribute to the search for the answer to these questions and the solution of all the known problems of society? Finally, what does society—its historical course, its present and future, its dangers and chances—mean for *theology?* Heinz-Dietrich Wendland and Dietrich von Oppen have taught us that human society and its forms of life are not a neutral realm for the gospel. Even before them, others risked more far-reaching statements, such as that of Rosenstock-Huessy: "Nature and society . . . are the fruits of the expansion of Christianity." "The Church has always seized even greater

65

portions of the creation away from the Devil. These new areas (to wit, the reunited creation) lie outside the Church, but they are not godless."[33] Or, as Dietrich Bonhoeffer wrote, challenging us to take seriously the presence of the crucified and risen Christ in the reality of the world: "In Christ we are offered the possibility of partaking in the reality of God and in the reality of the world, but not in one without the other. The reality of God discloses itself only by setting me entirely in the reality of the world, and when I encounter the reality of the world it is always already sustained, accepted, and reconciled in the reality of God."[34]

Even those who cannot follow one or the other of these contemporary theologians all the way will nevertheless have to admit that they have recognized and come to grips with a serious theological task that is still waiting to be taken up by most of the rest of us. After the decisive and necessary redirection of theology toward the *center* of the Lordship of Christ during the last forty years, we now have to be careful that we do not lose sight of the last forty years; we now have to be careful that we do not lose sight of the *horizons* of this Lordship[35] by unwittingly provincializing the Kingdom of the risen, victorious Lord to a sorry little Sunday precinct. We must dare to hope that he sends us not into the strangeness of a "godless" world, expecting us to "prove ourselves as Christians" in the midst of the confusing complexity of the hostile reality of the world, but, rather, that he is always ahead of us in the world in society, in business and commercial organizations, work and public life, politics and culture—at work in it as its risen Lord! As the Lord: that means we are always his co-workers in the world as those who may serve and suffer with him in concrete situations. The cross and resurrection of this Lord which is proclaimed and heard in the gathered congregations must be experienced in the world.

In this—New Testament!—sense we may now be "converted" to (i.e., turned toward) this our contemporary world. We may accept it as something he has accepted. What else could be expressed by this than our trust that *we* have been accepted by him?[36] In this trust we may look at the world with bright, not jaundiced, eyes, viewing it positively, not as a hostile country into which the church of Jesus Christ may occasionally send a missionary expedition, but instead, as the realm whose horizon is the good Lordship of the risen One, the realm in which God carries forward his mighty history.

Not only *opportunities* for the gospel but also its *effects* are to be discovered in the world of man. This is a fact of immense importance for the theologian. He need no longer think of himself as surrounded by powers that mock his sermons and make life difficult for him and his congregation. He learns instead to grasp the positive consequences of the gospel in things like "secularization," mobility, and in the organizational work that has freed many social relationships from irrational taboos. Thus, he finds himself and all Christians called to free and serene assumption of responsibility and personal engagement in these new forms of society.[37] Once he begins to understand that his Lord's presence is not confined to the realm of the church's speaking and acting, and begins to look over the fence of "church life" and to step outside it, he begins to find in an entirely new way that it is exciting and rewarding to be a theologian. To see this new joy awaken and grow is the most satisfying experience the leaders of the seminar have.

VI. Consequences: A Congregation Open to the World

It is hard for many a former seminar participant to prevent this new joy from being dampened by the reality of an official position in the present-day church. He returns to his office with new knowledge that he realizes requires some follow-through. But where in his office and in his congregation is there room for the sort of consequences demanded?

The first consequence required by the insights we have sketched here must be that the *congregation* be in the midst of the world and *open* for the world. Its distinctive features must not be only Sunday worship, weekday Bible classes, and

vertical differentiation into men's, women's, and youth groups
that no longer conform to the structure and group-forming
tendencies of contemporary society. Are not new characteris-
tics of Christian congregational structure imaginable in the
context of our complex, departmentalized society? Could there,
perhaps, be one evening for a meeting of employers and employees; another for discussion among educators, including
public-school teachers, masters in charge of the training of
apprentices for an industrial plant, and the traffic control in-
structor of the police force? A wealth of such possibilities are
available to our congregations, as has already been recognized
in many extra- and supra-congregational projects such as the
(lay) Evangelical Academies, student congregations, and in
work with industrial workers. Such measures could cause some
displacement within the structure of the congregation. New
faces would appear, and the worship service would be more
like a gathering of groups than of individuals. The pastor of
such a congregation would have to be able to listen to a great
many things, and have the time to think through theologically
the problems that come up. This means he will no longer be
able to do many of the things people expect from him as a
matter of course! But his role cannot be allowed to be de-
graded to that of an "official functionary" delivered up to
"attend" to the things people expect of such a person.[38] Much
has been written about this problem recently. Such books are
properly dealt with in the lectures at our seminar.[39] Here, we
desire only to point out the difficulty of drawing out the practical consequences from the insights of our intensive work in
the seminar, the difficulty of visualizing both the pastor and
his congregation in a new relationship to the world, a "diaconal
relationship" such as Heinz-Dietrich Wendland calls for.

VII. THEOLOGICAL DIACONATE—DIACONAL CONGREGATION

A diaconal relationship: this means that the congregation
should participate in the *diakonia* (service) of him who came
"not to be served but to serve." To take up this service means

at once "to have the same mind which Jesus Christ also had" (Phil. 2:5), and also to be converted from the attitude of an object to that of a subject, a serving witness to the *diakonia* of Jesus. To *speak* about it, and attest it in *words*, is one part of the service of witness. The other part is to *do* it in the form of concrete, responsible service in contemporary society.[40]

At this point we have to face the question whether our equation "theologian = parish minister" has not been taken too much for granted.[41] A diaconal relationship of the church to the world demands many theologians who will not be parish ministers but will, rather, be free for and commissioned to the task of theological reflection upon the practical problems of society. We need theologians who are at the disposal of the groups and institutions of social life in order to offer their special kind of assistance, which economists, sociologists, psychologists, jurists, technicians, and doctors alone cannot provide. Such extraecclesiastical service unfortunately has the reputation of "unfaithfulness" (so many pastorates are vacant!), and in some cases even arouses the accusation of betrayal of the essential concern of the church. As if this sort of service were not precisely a special way of implementing the "essential concern" of the church! Hans-Ruedi Weber, of the Department of the Laity of the World Council of Churches, pointed out, in an unpublished paper, the curious fact that in France at a meeting of Protestant theologians the people who held important positions of responsibility in social life were regarded as being "on vacation from church service." Is an essential theological service to be regarded as a "vacation" from church service? Must we not, on the contrary, ordain such theologians and send them into such service?

Would such a social diaconate be possible on the basis of our parish congregations? *Must* such service originate from that point? Conflicting opinions may be heard on this issue. Up till now we in the seminar believe we must answer with a "both . . . and." The sociologist warns us, to be sure: "As long as the structure of society exhibited relatively closed

69

living areas it was possible to reflect and to shape it in the local congregation. Since these areas began to be broken up, without changing the shape of the local congregation, however, the old possibility of reflecting the society has largely been lost, even in the countryside. This has led, on the one hand, to core groups of those who live on the periphery of social change, and on the other hand, to an exodus from the local congregations of all those who are caught in this breakup. . . . As long as we persist in speaking today about the legally established local congregation as a sociologically significant unit, we indulge in a fiction which will have dangerous consequences."[42] Can we bear to hear the conclusion of a sociologist? Do we think it through, or do we push it aside as a bother, if possible with the judgment that it is "incompetent"? "The present local congregation can no longer play a direct role in the transmission of the Gospel or as the primary form of faith."[43]

We do not wish, in the face of such conclusions, to advocate as the alternative the so-called "paracongregation," which since Evanston has been spirited about in church meetings and discussions as a kind of apparition. Rather, our concern is seriously to raise the question about the possibility of a *transformation* of the traditional local congregation, *and* at the same time, without waiting for an answer to the first question, asking whether new congregations ought to grow up alongside the old ones, particularly in new industrial areas and housing developments, the distinctive marks of which will from the outset be those of the social diaconate described above and not those of pastorally "caring for" and spiritually "tending" a specific number of souls. These should be congregations whose members do not flee from the world into a religiously appointed Sunday space, but, rather, after they have taken hold of and worked upon the problems and questions arising in the everyday life of the world, seek to test and answer them against the witness of the Bible and in prayer, and are thus constantly moving toward the world.

VIII. Not Just the Music of the Future

A few such congregations *do exist*—with the full consent of the church authorities. We are thinking especially of those places in which former seminar members are working: in the "Ark" in Wolfsburg, the Volkswagen city; in the Baunatal project in Kassel; in Gelsenkirchen-Buer-Hassel in the Ruhr. It is significant that these experiments—for that is all they are![44]—have been undertaken at completely ordinary focal points of industry, and not in those disjointed places of "social need." What is happening here is in no sense ecclesiastical emergency work. A new type of congregation should be developed in relatively advanced but no less normal situations for the majority of our congregations in our time and in the near future, suited especially for witness to the Lordship of Jesus Christ in our society by means of *kērygma, diakonia,* and *koinōnia.*[45] Above all, a transformation of the relationship between theologians and laymen will have to be accomplished in these congregations. The laity must no longer be assistants who help the pastor perform his service, but just the opposite. They are the ones whose business is, according to Eph. 4:12, "the work of ministry," the circle of those who are concerned with pertinent, responsible service in the world.[46] This fundamental initial change calls for others to follow in its wake, however, as will be briefly indicated below. These first came to light among the members of our seminar while they were living together at Gossner Haus with seventy young workers, apprentices, students, and foreign interns, and having many encounters with men in the neighborhood.[47]

In all gatherings, even at Sunday morning worship, everyone present is called upon to raise questions, to answer to the others, and to pray. There is no theological or spiritual monopoly. Baptism, which is occasionally performed in this "model" congregation at the request of the participants and with the approval of the local pastor, is a matter for the whole congregation. They have deliberated for long hours among them-

71

selves and with the parents and godparents about the justifica-
tion, the intention, and the right understanding of this act.
Thus, Baptism is not accepted as a mere customary rite, but as
a weighty event that raises questions and demands practical
consequences. The Lord's Supper, which is celebrated weekly
at the table used for daily meals, is set up in the midst of
everyday life and there constitutes the communion between
the Lord of the world and the remnant seated around the
table, and at the same time creates fellowship among the
celebrants and strengthens them for service in the church and
in the world.[48] After the preaching of the death and resurrection of the Lord, the members help one another through their
conversation around the table to understand their common
tasks and common service.[49]

IX. Ecclesia Semper Reformanda

The members of the seminar, who come not only from Germany but from all over the world, are thoroughly critical and
by no means accept everything "new" that they see and hear
in Gossner Haus. But they recognize a possibility of church
service and church fellowship in our age, which they previously had no inkling about. The blinkers of a constricted
confessional viewpoint and a limited social horizon are torn
away. One begins to get ideas and to imagine: "Thou settest
my feet upon a wide land." Is it a great shame when the *élan*
the young theologian receives here appears to shoot beyond
the target once in a while, so that their fellow pastors and
church superintendents feel uneasy? No one wishes to "shock
at any price." And is there anything better than when theologians are ablaze for the good cause of the gospel? The danger
consists much more in the possibility that this blaze will one
day be quenched because the church is hermetically sealed
against the entrance of fresh air, and new experiences of the
Holy Spirit are dampened by self-complacency fed with the
pious-sounding argument about being the "servant of the little
flock," which is in reality one of the worst enemies of the

Holy Spirit. To reckon with him as a real force in the "economy" of the church means today to will a new congregation capable of working out its obedience to the old, original commission of the church precisely in the midst of this new, rapidly changing world. In the Church of the Reformation, the *ecclesia semper reformanda*,[50] this view ought to be neither heresy nor sacrilege.

The Seminar for the Church's Service in Industry—now, more accurately, in Industrial Society—would like its work to provide our theologians with *courage* to serve in an as yet largely unknown, intellectually unplowed world, which is rapidly pulling away from us. Precisely its mobility offers us our greatest chances, for just here it awaits our service: "The transmission of God's forgiveness to every man in the midst of everyday life and work is the calling of Christians around the world, their unique and inalienable apostolate."[51] If the seminar and those who have passed through its courses are able to assist in this apostolate, it has fulfilled its purpose.

73

PART II. THE RENEWAL OF THE CHURCH FOR ITS
              SERVICE IN THE WORLD

4

RECOVERY OR SENILITY?

THE PATIENT is the church. Is she improving or is she done for? Will her health be restored by injections of evangelistic campaigns, or home-missions tablets, and removal to the better lighted and better ventilated spaces of modern church buildings? Jazz music in the worship service, catchy themes placed before the public eye with all the techniques of modern advertising, Bible texts and prayers camouflaged as newspaper ads—all this reminds one of the type of aging woman who desires to give the impression of life in full bloom by means of a little hastily applied makeup. All this is unworthy of the church of Jesus Christ. It was always the church's best time when she acknowledged her illness, confessed it to the Lord, and admitted it to the world. But the evangelical churches of Western vintage seem to be taking King Asa as their patron saint, of whom II Chron. 16:12 tells us that when he was suffering from a foot disease, "he did not seek the Lord in his sickness, but sought the physicians instead." It is by no means easy to place oneself in the hands of that one Physician, since he desires the most energetic cooperation of the patient. "If you listen to the voice of the Lord your God, heed and do what is right before him, and give ear to all his commandments and keep all his laws, then I will not lay upon you any of the diseases which I laid upon Egypt, because I am the Lord, your physician." (Ex. 15:26.) But so many other physicians stand around our patient, the church, bidding her to accept government subsidies and other well-meant remedies, for example, that she forgets the seriousness of her illness and manages despite her senility (Respect the aged!) to look quite respectable to herself.

But the church has the promise of recovery—indeed, of becoming youthful (Isa. 40:29 ff.). The condition for such recovery is that she give up treatments with quack remedies and become completely the patient of her only physician, the Lord. For he is not merely a doctor who prescribes remedies but one who suffers with his patient, shares her weakness, and does not withdraw in shame from his weak church like those men who turn up their noses at her or point their fingers at her in contempt. He stands in solidarity with his patient, becomes a sufferer himself, a "patient."[52] In doing this, he shows the church how in the midst of suffering he is not preoccupied with himself but is there for the sake of serving others. The church will regain her health and become "a city set on a hill" when she ceases being preoccupied with herself and her self-preservation. Otherwise, she will surely lose her life despite or because of her countless expensive church construction projects and her imposing mass meetings. Even if the number of sermons preached on Sundays were doubled, their quality improved, the congregations reduced in size, and the number of congregations and ordained personnel multiplied, the decisive factor would still have to be added: the task of the church in the world. The church will become stronger and build herself up anew when she comes to grips with this task.

Precisely at this point the church is failing, however. Congregations see no task for them in the surrounding society. Whenever one asks a pastor and the members of his congregation about such a task, the answers one receives always refer to some sort of intraecclesiastical work: church construction, developing more closely knit congregations, inviting outsiders, or providing a shot in the arm for the faithful. Contact with broad social problems usually occurs for the first time in these conversations in expressions of concern for building day camps and homes for children, the youth, and the aged. But these are concerns which have long since been recognized by society. It may seriously be questioned whether Christian congregations ought to spend time, energy, and money to create church institutions of this type.

At one time that was necessary, e.g., when Johannes Evangelista Gossner, during the first half of the nineteenth century when Berlin was becoming industrialized, gave birth through his preaching to the first "child protection society" and a "society for visitation of the sick." Out of such beginnings there then developed, as happened in other places too under the initiative of Christians, great deaconess homes and the hospitals tended by them.

Today, society knows that it may not leave the sick uncared for. It accepts this responsibility and does not need to be reminded by the churches that it has this duty. Evidence for this can be found, for example, in the fact that even in the East extensive health programs are maintained by the socialist states. In some parts of the world the special initiative and example of Christians are still needed to stir men to recognition and acceptance of their responsibility for sickness and need. There was good reason for the Gossner Mission to lay the cornerstone of a hospital in Amgaon, India, in 1956, and to send doctors and nurses there. When the people of India have recognized this task as their own, however, the people sent by the mission can return and even the Indian Christians will also be able to turn their attention to new tasks. The church should always hold a service of thanksgiving when the "world" takes over part of the work formerly done by it. The church should not complain about losing another piece of its work. The world does not need to become a sort of church or be "Christianized." Instead, it should be stimulated to take up necessary tasks by the pioneering and exemplary work of

79

Christians. Christian congregations would simply have to be concerned that a spirit of love and responsibility reigns among their members, for this is what makes Christians ready to commit themselves for the sake of other men. They will have to work courageously and without thanks precisely in those callings which involve caring for the sick and the exploited. They will have to enter organizations that fight for the rights of the weak. They will become honorary co-workers with the local social security agencies, the educational institutions, and the municipal authorities. The goal of *every* congregation should be the creation of men of contagious humanity, with a high sense of responsibility, and the ability to spend themselves selflessly for the needs and tasks of society.

In the complexity of modern society, what is needed is readiness for social involvement not only on the part of individuals but on the part of groups as well. An individual may well recognize that some job has to be done, but he can do this job only by working together with other individuals. For this reason, the congregation ought to be divided more and more into *service groups*, which are set up to undertake specific tasks that are of limited scope and that require a limited amount of time for completion. They should not be set up in perpetuity, but should be dissolved when their work is done or proves to be beyond their capacity. The picture of the "congregation of the future" should not be dominated by "circles" (for which one is always seeking and for the most part not finding things to do) but, rather, by special, temporary service groups.

Examples of such groups may be found both in the East and in the West. In an industrial city one group became concerned about the so-called "key kids,"[53] who either hung around together on the streets or else remained alone at home waiting for their parents to return from work. This sort of concern began when a few members of such a group started to play with these children, and helped them to do their schoolwork. It led to conversation with the parents, discussions with the social departments of the city and industry, and to serious reflection upon the entire system of social, political, and economic organization in our society. This one small example already shows that the congregation as a whole is challenged.

The sort of group needed here requires not just a few persons of goodwill but, above all, persons of this type who also have a competent understanding of the problems and the necessary ability to deal with them. These problems must be formulated and thought through, and specific posts and organizations in society alerted which, disturbed and stimulated by the initiative of such service groups, will themselves assume responsibility for these problems and for carrying on the work. Anyone who wishes to work within confessional boundaries will soon be left behind in such work. Service groups like these operating in the social order must be open to Christians of all shades, also to humanists and atheists. Anyone should be allowed to work in them who desires to move beyond the *status quo*, and who refuses to sanction the old order but desires meaningful change for the sake of human welfare.

What the special contribution of Christians will be to such efforts cannot be predicted. That will have to be seen in the course of healthy competition between the Christians, the humanists, and the atheists. It would already be a signal witness to the authenticity of their Christian existence if they would show their confidence with more patience and perseverance and not grow weary of making sacrifices or despair of final victory while working to open up the possibility of change for the better. This sort of thing would be not only a good contribution toward getting the work done but would be at the same time a testimony to the fact that there really is something in their faith in the resurrection. The assertion that Jesus Christ lives and changes this world has very little influence upon men today no matter how often it is repeated. When Christians step into social problems and learn the meaning of the cross and resurrection in the midst of bearing the burdensome problems of everyday life, then they will really become witnesses to their Lord. Then even their companions of other persuasions will see that for them the issue is not the preservation of a little flock of pious people and their church organization but, rather, the healing of their world. The hope of Christians can be that contagious. There is no reason why they have to look like the taillight of society when they are called to be the light of the world.

Up till now we have not spoken about the theologians and the ordained officials of the church. They will be neither the decisive members nor the leaders in these service groups. The laity, that is, the members of the *laos* (I Peter 2:9), the people of God, are called to bear witness to the mighty acts of God. Such witness does not need to be limited to verbal communication but may be expressed in the sort of witness described above. Christian witness has a triadic form which includes preaching, service, and fellowship (*kērygma, diakonia, koinōnia*). If one omits any one of these three, the witness is ineffective. In German theology, preaching has become absolutized, diaconal service limited to charitable work, and fellowship regarded as a sign of a sect. The proper coordination of these three things is the task of the future theology and practice of the church.

The service group demands unconditional fellowship among its members if it is to complete its task. Experience teaches that they will need just as much to listen together to the "commands and laws" mentioned above (*supra,* pp. 77–78). Confronted with a concrete problem, even those members of the group who remain outside the church will be willing to listen to the exhortation and promise of the Bible if these actually help to point the way to the goal. A general exposition, oriented perhaps to the text for Sunday, will be uninteresting to them. They do not take it for granted that a text from the Bible is "the Word of God." But they can be grasped and set moving by a Biblical text if it bears upon the work of this group. Christians in the group will always be on the lookout for such possibilities of filling up the fuel tank again after it has run dry. All too often the fuel provided by the churches is like that which one obtained at carriage stations in the past, so that today one has to pass the church by because even with the best of intentions he cannot get his motor to run on oats and water. Even today's motors are not all alike. One needs gasoline; another, diesel fuel; another, a mixture. Where is one to get the proper fuel?

Undoubtedly, the Sunday worship of the congregation for many years was the source of strength for service in the social order. For many men this is still the spring from which they draw such strength. After the First World War, group Bible study rooted in the experiences of the Pietists, gained in significance. The climax of this movement was reached in the Confessing Church. Both these forms of transmitting the power of service were dominated by the person of the theologian, who was at once shepherd and pastor. Today it has become evident that the theologian can no longer play such a role in a service group.

The laity themselves often prove to be better suited for the service of shepherds and pastors, especially since they are continually called upon to provide this sort of service in their vocational work, associations, and—as was the case in the past too—in their families. They cannot withdraw into a small shell of their own private certainty and expectation of salvation, because in every step in their vocational work they are called upon to cooperate with one man after another. They are asked every minute about the significance of Jesus Christ for themselves as his disciples, as well as for the other men and for the group as a whole. They stand on a battle line: they are challenged and must fight and respond. They cannot have recourse to "the" church and its ordained officials. *They* are the church and *they* have the office of carrying on the ministry of reconciliation (II Cor. 5:18). Questions arise unceasingly in the pursuit of this work. They are addressed to the Christians by those outside the church, and they arise from within the Christian himself. How far may reconciliation extend?

83

Might it not lead to a rotten peace? Should Christian involvement for the sake of a fellowman be persisted in even when it becomes dangerous for one's person? Are the present arrangements of superiors and subordinates, distribution and exercise of power, property, and production, etc., just? Or does the gospel demand their alteration, perhaps even their dissolution? How should the fruit of our labors be distributed in the plant, in the nation, and among the nations? What do we have to say about surplus food on one side and hunger on the other? Does the danger of nuclear warfare allow Christians to remain passive, or does it, rather, call "the peacemakers" into the arena of political activity? Where does the Lord want to see his disciples today? Where should they become involved to become his fellow workers?

These are concrete questions which do not permit of generalized answers. The precise answers can be worked out only by the questioner and the one questioned. For this reason, dialogue between them is necessary. *Theologians* may be drawn into this dialogue so that their scientific, academic, specialized knowledge may assist the others in thinking through their questions. That is the legitimate task for which the theologian has studied to prepare himself. One example may clarify our thesis.

When universal military training was proclaimed in East Germany in January, 1962, six young married couples who met regularly as a "house church" discussed the meaning of this law for themselves and their companions. The latter had immediately begun to ask them what they ought to say and what their attitude should be in the face of this issue. Some of them had given various answers, although all of them seemed inadequate at that moment. Some of them had remained silent. What did Jesus Christ demand of them in that situation? Should they keep still? How should they decide when their orders to report for duty arrived? After two hours their conversation came to a standstill, without anyone, not even the two pastors who were present, knowing what he should say or do about it. Then a young married woman suggested that they celebrate the Lord's Supper. The head of the house brought in from the kitchen a slice of bread on a dish and a glass of wine, looked around the circle, and handed both to an engineer. "You do it," he said. The engineer asked how it should be done. One of the pastors handed him a Bible opened to I Cor., ch. 11. He read the words of institution. Those present ate and drank, and each one prayed, calling out from the depths like the psalmist. And they gave thanks. Then they continued to converse about the same issue, now with a bit more hope and confidence and a little less anxiety. As midnight approached, the members of the group asked these questions of the theologians:

1. Do the Old and the New Testaments say the same or different things about war and military service?

2. How did the early Christian community relate itself to these things? Did they tolerate soldiers in their midst, or were there Christians who were also soldiers?

3. How was it possible for there to be a complete reversal of policy on these matters during the time of Constantine? Did they simply substitute a different set of Bible proof texts?

4. What did the Reformers, not only Luther but also Zwingli and Calvin, say about military service?

5. Have the positions and pronouncements of the Synods of the Evangelical Church in Germany during the last decade been consistent or inconsistent on the subjects of rearmament, peace, and war? What have the synods of the territorial churches said, and what position has our own territorial church taken?

6. How did the so-called "peace churches" arise? What are their main arguments for refusing to enter military service? What experiences have they had in this regard?

7. What are the laws in other countries? What possibilities do they offer?

Not one in the group thought of asking the pastors what he should do. That would be asking too much of the theologians. They could not exempt anyone from making his own decision. But the theologians had now received their task, which was to make it possible for the group to meet again in a week and come to a clearer understanding of the issues so that each person could reach his own decision.

The shoemaker has to stick to his last, the theologian to his theology. The purpose of his theological education was to enable him to take up the questions of a group like this and to think them through, perhaps in collaboration with the historian or whoever else he might need. He is not needed for the administration of the Lord's Supper. Now everyone in that group knows where the words of institution are to be found. But he is indeed needed when it comes to grappling with Biblical and historical questions, and for information about current developments. How long must the theologian work on the task of answering these questions? Results were desired within a week because time was short. Answers and decisions could not be tabled. The theologian is so important to this group as an assistant that they provide his living. They need him with his knowledge in order to be able to exist as "church" in present-day society.

This example is meant to illustrate the things for which theologians should be used. They are utterly misused today when they are set to tasks that are not within their province. These include not only administrative matters, such as construction of churches, nurseries, homes for the aged, and parsonages. Things such as house calls, burials, and perhaps even baptism and the other special acts usually associated with the pastoral office should also be included here. Luther could say with reference to the preacher: "He may . . . leave baptizing and such minor offices to others, as Christ did, and St. Paul, and all the apostles (Acts, ch. 6)."[54] The theologian should take himself seriously as a theologian. Each Christian, as a living member of the body of Christ, has his specific functions. They are not mere pendants that make a few wobbly motions when struck by the theologian. It is not so much prattle when the congregation confesses its faith in the Holy Spirit and believes in his action. But the congregation must also seek out men within it who are well grounded in Biblical faith and equipped with a solid "lay theology," and who will be in a position to visit a home in bereavement over a death, and to pray with the people in it and to say the right words at the grave. The work of the theologian comes in at the point of equipping the members of his congregation, not at the burial itself, which in large cities would keep him scurrying back and forth from the crematory to the cemetery. The same applies to other special acts and duties of the pastoral office. The separation of "spiritual men" and "laymen" is unbiblical and therefore unevangelical: "For no one can deny that every Christian has God's Word and is taught of God and anointed by Him to be a priest."[55] There are different functions to be performed in a congregation. The theologian can by no means combine all in his person: "And God should not be tempted with requests to send a new preacher from heaven. Rather, we must betake ourselves to Scripture and call from among ourselves those whom we find suited for this work."[56] And if current church ordinances oppose this view? Then, "we must hold ourselves to Scripture" and change the others.

The theologian must be free to pursue the specific work he has been charged with. The equation "theologian = shepherd and pastor" will not do. There are many hidden shepherds and pastors among the members of the congregation who ought to be given official authorization. This is even more the case in connection with the various functions that laymen carry out in the secular world. The chairman of an industrial council, responsible for thousands of men, will be asked by Christ in exactly the same way as an ordained pastor what he has done with the men who have come to his office seeking help. Did he offer them cheap comfort, transfer them to another place, and in the next moment forget all about them, taking up the "next case"? Or did he suffer with them, and lose sleep because the problems of these others would not let him rest? Secular

87

shepherding and pastoral care is perhaps all the more difficult because it is so often deprived of a source of strength. What might it mean if theologians could be assistants to these secular pastors not only in our churches but even more in our modern society?

Of course, if they are to do this, their university work must have already provided them with a theology oriented toward contemporary society. It will not be enough simply to advise theological students to take a little sociology, economics, psychology, philosophy, education, etc. It should not be up to the students to bake the theological loaf from such different ingredients taken in varying amounts. The theological professors themselves must do this, for only on this basis do they have any right to continue to teach at a "university." If the theological professors do not do the job of confronting the other disciplines, no other theologians can be expected to do it. Critical exegesis of the Bible and investigations in the area of church history have already changed as a result of their encounter with modern studies. Theology has yet to do the same with other modern disciplines, especially sociology, economics, and education. Demands upon the theologians are growing rapidly in our society. Theology will be able to do justice to them only if the theological faculties keep pace with modern developments.

Opportunities are waiting for Christians in the tasks presented by the contemporary world. In order for these to be seen and taken up by the churches we need a theology that is open to the world; theologians rich in knowledge of the world; church members who gladly assume responsibility in pioneering, working service groups; and congregations prepared to make changes. Everywhere the results of New Delhi should be carefully noted and studied, and courageously put into practice. We are much farther along in these matters at the level of the ecumenical movement today than we are in the individual churches and congregations. We must push ahead if the church is to recover and not sink into senility.

5

CONGREGATION WITHOUT PULPIT

THERE are many pulpits around. Many of them are so high above the congregation that the preacher is unable to determine, even if he has good eyes, whether his words are causing smirks or sadness among the people far below. The listeners are addressed as "brothers" and "sisters"; and one counts on the fact that here the "beloved congregation"[57] is gathered. Theoretically this may be true, and there are good theological grounds for such an assumption. But practically speaking, there is little indication that here a congregation of brothers and sisters is gathered. It makes one very sad to hear of some students who, no longer able to bear the anonymity of being mere visitors at the worship service of a local parish, followed hard upon the heels of one of the members of the congregation, grabbed him by the arm, and said: "We beg your pardon, but we were at the worship service and would like to introduce ourselves. May we accompany you for a short distance?" The reaction was, to say the least, astonishment, and even indignation, and withdrawal. "It is absolutely none of their business to ask who I am and where I worship."

It was on the Sunday before "Mad Monday"[58] of this year that a pastor of the Seminar for the Church's Service in Industrial Society, who had been working for weeks in an industrial plant on the day shift as well as the night shift, roused himself on a work-free Sunday and went to morning worship.

89

He longed for fellowship under the Word, for common prayer and praise to God. He had brought with him a hymnal that, unfortunately, was not the one used by the churches in this region. The liturgy was unknown to him, and he could discover no one who seemed to take an interest in this stranger. In that great church building, each person, especially the married couples, stood at a distance of at least three meters from his neighbors. The preacher spoke on the text for that Sunday, I Cor., ch. 13, the great hymn of love. He began by saying that this love creates fellowship both with God, the vertical dimension, and among men, the horizontal dimension. It does not exist in one dimension without at the same time existing in the other. Now, our pastor felt that he was not in a position to verify the former, but the latter seemed very dubious to him in the case of this congregation. This impression was strengthened when at the close of the worship service everyone went off in his own direction without in the least concerning himself with the others. As this pastor went his own way, he came to a corner where a crowd of swaying people were singing carnival songs. And he was even more confused because it seemed to him that here, in a peculiarly caricatured way, the latter (i.e., love for fellowmen) seemed to be present. If it really is the case that the two dimensions of love belong inseparably together, then the presence of a pulpit seems to be no certain guarantee that the congregation gathered beneath it is really a fellowship between men in the sense of I Cor., ch. 13. Conversely, it may well be that a congregation, in the full sense, can arise without ever once sitting under a pulpit and listening to a sermon in the ordinary sense.

For more than five years some fellow workers at the plant kept asking me when I was going to quit my work as a laborer and once again become a genuine pastor. Did I really like it so well being among them? they would ask. I honestly could affirm that I did like it up to a particular point: "You hold that what I say from the pulpit on Sunday is foolishness; you assert that it doesn't interest you. But up till now not a single one of you has come to me and offered to help me so

that I could make my sermons better and more interesting."
After some head-shaking, three of my fellow workers declared
themselves ready to meet with me on Friday evening, and
together with a young pastor who also worked at the same
plant, they would help me prepare the sermon for the following Sunday. Since then we have met regularly. In the mean-
time, our circle has grown to more than twenty in number.
None of these men go to church, not even to the church in
which I myself have to preach from time to time. They don't
listen to what they themselves have produced. That place is
strange to them, and the manner in which people conduct
themselves there is just as strange. Some years ago a co-worker
did take it upon himself to go to church on Easter Sunday.
The following Tuesday, as we entered the plant, he greeted
me and said: "Hey, I had to laugh when you came out of
that box (i.e., the pulpit!); and the things you said I couldn't
understand at all. What do you mean, 'Jesus lives and changes
the world'?"

This conversation continued and lasted far beyond that
week. What really does change, say, in an unhappy family
life; among the nations of this vast world; in the factory,
between employer and employees; in my pay envelope? The
questions that are pointed at pulpit assertions like that one are
very "worldly" and concrete. An answer to them can be worked
out only together, through conversation. We have to find new
similes and parables, meaningful images and words, taken
from the already existing environment of these modern men,
which will make it possible for them to realize what we are
talking about. Thus, the sermon preparation that we do in
our study is only a beginning, a first step. This must be followed by conversation, and this not with the good members
of our congregation who all too readily nod assent. Much more
helpful are those who say "No" and who compel the preacher
to say things far more clearly and concretely. Contradiction
at the point of the birth and formation of a sermon will prevent
it from taking dogmatic shortcuts and becoming tiresome to
listen to.

91

Above all, such conversation will bring out, perhaps for the first time, what questions our contemporaries are really asking. Too many theologians seem to have no regard for this matter. They are of the opinion that God alone asks and answers the questions. He asks and answers through the Word of Holy Scripture. Man has to allow himself to be questioned by God and then listen to God's answer. Whoever doesn't fit into this scheme stays outside. And in fact many people do stand outside, more than those who stand within. Thus do an unbelievable number of pulpit broadcasters transmit their questions and answers over this schematized wavelength into the—yes, whence?—into the world or into their congregations. In any case, many people lack the proper receiving apparatus for this wavelength and therefore cannot be reached by this kind of transmission. Moreover, God himself took man more seriously than these theologians do. Otherwise, he wouldn't have walked the earth in the man Jesus of Nazareth. He actually did ask: "What do you want me to do?"[59]

We, too, must seek opportunities to put such questions and to search together for the answers. We would then discover that a Biblical text which is meaningful and exciting to a preacher may leave other men completely cold. We would discover this in a moment by reading the Beatitudes. In the case of our circle, the conversation labored tortuously over the first two Beatitudes. Strange as it may seem, neither the poor nor the mournful were actually represented in this group of men from the industrial world. But we had hardly touched upon the epigram about the meek who are to inherit the earth when the discussion caught fire. Here we had come up against a verse above which one could well place a sign: "Caution! Dangerous explosive!" Here all the silently suppressed and disturbing questions which these men carried about concerning their daily bread, the factory hierarchy or bureaucracy, the life of their neighborhood, and the world of the nations—all these questions were unearthed at this point. With this Beatitude, the whole question of a competitive economic system as such, as well as the smaller issues of competitive struggle within such a system, were brought to consciousness and formulated. This verse not only brought out a hundred new questions, however, but also put us in a position in which we found ourselves questioned by the verse. Thus a master from one of the industrial plants answered, "Tomorrow I am going to try to operate with this meekness in relation to the matter we have discussed, since it seems to me to offer a real and new possibility." Then I felt like the pastor in Ernst Wiechert's novel *The Simple Life*, who said to his nocturnal visitor: "I know that such a verse has waited until it was time. Do you understand?"

So we need space in which we can talk to one another. Everyone must have the opportunity to express himself with regard to what he has heard, to put his questions and also to register his dissent. The "No" does not need to be banned from the congregation, but, on the contrary, must be allowed to have its place within its walls, just as in the early Christian church the "Amen" to the sermon could be either spoken out or withheld by the congregation. Probably someone would want to rebuke such expressions of opinion at official gatherings of the congregation, such as the so-called Bible class (*Bibelstunde*). It is true that it is at just this sort of gathering, where the inner core of our congregations comes together and by asking questions comes to a fuller understanding of the text, that such expressions of doubt and contradiction *cannot* in fact be expected.

Where in our churches is there a place where faith is not presupposed, where, on the contrary, it is assumed that faith will have to be awakened by speaking together? Where are the Christians who place themselves alongside other men who bend under the burden of their nonunderstanding and counterarguments? To get down to a very practical point: we need Christian gatherings that are not opened and closed by the singing of a hymn. Many people who don't know these hymns are made to feel extremely uncomfortable by this procedure. Our conversation—our spoken prayers with an invisible Other —is an extremely alienating matter for those who do not know this "Invisible Partner" of our conversation. They feel completely outside our circle under these circumstances. Probably they will never return again. But it is absolutely unnecessary to set up the situation in such a way that these people always feel they are being addressed ex cathedra, or instructed and straightened out like schoolchildren.

In academic circles, where it is a matter of scholarship and learning, there is a place for teaching chairs. But there is no place for such things when it is a matter of understanding my life and death. On such matters, I want to have something to say. I do not assume that a given teaching authority already possesses the answers, but I want first to get acquainted with this authority in order to decide whether or not I can follow it. Unfortunately, our church buildings, with their bolted-down pews, allow for no conversation with the man in the pulpit, or even between the people in the congregation. They seem to be designed to compel one to look in only one direction, just as the seats in a movie do. The analogy of the movie house is complete when the practice is adopted of dimming the lights as the sermon begins, so that only the pulpit light remains lighted. In the Catholic Church such a procedure is quite appropriate and justified. But how does this procedure fit into an Evangelical Church? In my opinion we are still building our churches in a Catholic fashion, despite the new efforts being made in church architecture.

Wherever men gather together to talk with one another they place themselves in a circle: we often name such groups "circles." In a circle everyone has the same right: no one is elevated above the rest. Everyone has the same chance if he opens his mouth. The one who puts the brakes on the conversation by his contradictions helps to achieve an ever greater depth and clarity. This is all for the benefit of understanding the Word of the text. Is it any wonder that our conversation partners say: "You cannot tell us any more from the pulpit on Sunday than we have already learned here"? Above all, the question of concrete action can be brought up here in a manner entirely different from that in a sermon. Everyday situations can be depicted, and the concrete decisions they put before us can be expressed. Then we pastors can see the extent to which we have only the most general understanding of what we preach, and how little we know how to apply the Word of the Bible to concrete cases.

Often the clarifying and helpful word comes from someone who is still raising all kinds of questions and contradictions, and yet, sometimes he, as the only one or as the first one, is able to point the way on the basis of this Word. Here, in a happy fashion, it turns out that the other man is by no means merely the object to whom the Biblical questions and answers are to be addressed, but, rather, that he, in the counterposing of his questions and answers against those of the Word of God, is turned into a brother who goes along a common path with us. Now we help one another side by side through the briers of everyday life. We ask about one another and visit one another. They admit, somewhat ashamedly, that many things have changed in their relationships with one another and even with other men. They abhor any kind of labeling, the churches' most of all. They haven't become a congregation gathered around a pulpit. But haven't they indeed become a congregation in which the Word of God stands in their midst, as something that has become interesting, exciting, and explosive for them, and from which they receive the answer to their questions?

I hear the objection: songs of praise, prayer, Baptism, and the Lord's Supper also belong to a congregation. It is not the purpose of this talk to discuss these matters. Someone will point out that we have conducted baptisms. Yes, but we by no means took for granted the "Yes" of the parents and godparents, or even of those who were baptized (in cases where they were grown persons) in doing this. Even the sacrament of Baptism was risked and made a matter of discussion among us. The meal that we eat after the baptism can get cold as far as we are concerned, but the matter is discussed. Those who participate in the baptism, i.e., the one baptized, or the parents and godparents, must first be able to say what they hold concerning baptism, what their understanding of the church is, what they affirm and what they deny. Regarding the celebration of the Lord's Supper, we have no altar with a pastor in front of it, but instead, a circle of tables such as we use for our daily meals, festively set for this occasion, and with men sitting at them also dressed as if for a festive occasion. The texts are read now from one table, now from another; the prayers are short and natural, relating to daily life; the bread and wine are passed around from hand to hand, sometimes being passed on without being eaten or drunk by the person doing the passing—sometimes because of still unresolved questions, sometimes because he belongs to a different confession. Church ordinances are quite simple and straightforward so long as one can count on 100 percent agreement among the members, or does not allow their diversity to come out into the open! But such ordinances do not agree with life, as becomes evident as soon as one steps outside the sheltered area of tradition and convention. Only when this or that person passes on the bread and wine without partaking of them, or another takes only the bread and passes on the chalice, does one notice that the Lord's Supper too is a place where decision is called for just as much as the Third Beatitude.

There are many pulpits around us. But there are too few congregations without pulpits. This is not the place for polemics. We desire only to make it possible for many men to have easier access to the Word of God and to the Sacraments. And we would make it easier if we could invite them to a place where there was no pulpit but where a congregation was present nevertheless. The pastors, too, would have great joy in such congregations. The world would appear to them in an entirely new light, as a field ripe for harvest awaiting the harvesters. They would no longer be lonely figures, but would know that they really had brothers and sisters at their side who would allow themselves to be sent along with them into the harvest field of the world.

6

CONGREGATION WITHOUT WALLS

God always finds ways to move his church to the place at which it has to fulfill its commission. The church has often in its history balked at this commission and attempted to withdraw behind its walls in order to keep busy with itself alone. Then God battered down these walls, not with the intent of destroying the church, but, rather, to set it in motion once again toward the goal *he* had set for it. Thus we are told in The Acts of the Apostles: "Those who were now scattered went about preaching the Word" (Acts 8:4).

A Christian congregation must therefore not live self-sufficiently for itself. It gathers to listen to the Word of its Lord, but in the next minute it must disperse into the houses and neighborhoods, the vocations and organizations, in order to pass on what was heard and to transmute it into action. This is continually happening with all of you! Moreover, you remain a congregation throughout this process: you are never outside the church. You simply assume another form of the congregation of Jesus Christ, namely, the dispersed congregation, the Christian diaspora in the world.

A motor cannot run on one stroke alone. It needs at least a second. It produces power only through the two-stroke cycle of intake and explosion. Similarly, the congregation lives in the double movement of gathering and dispersing. Only in this way can it be a genuine congregation and perform the service it is commissioned to render in the world. Every attempt to withdraw behind the walls of the church and leave the world to go its own way indicates impotence and stagnation. Our congregational life will become boring and unreal if it lacks orientation toward the questions and problems of the world. God does not allow us any spiritual self-complacency, not even if we garnish it with Biblical phrases, church traditions, and ceremony. He loved the *world* and desires that the world know something of this love. He wills to use his congregation to this end. It is his instrument. A tool must, of course, be kept in good condition. The congregation can remain an instrument only if it continually allows itself to be kept in condition by God. This happens when it gathers for the Word and Sacrament. Then God is present, sharpening and dressing out his instrument so that it will be useful for his work in the world. A congregation that wanted to get along without this service of God [i.e., worship; *Gottesdienst*] would soon become a blunt, useless instrument, a piece of worn-out iron that will be thrown onto the world's gigantic ideological scrapheap.

Thus, we must speak about the twofold form of the life of the congregation of Jesus Christ: its life as gathered congregation, and its service as dispersed in the world.

We begin with the latter. Who is supposed to perform this service in the world in God's name? The pastor and the church superintendent, by means of press releases and church publicity? The welfare secretaries[60] and parish workers, deacons and deaconesses? No, this is not a matter for the Christians in the "chief official positions." *All of you* who are baptized and who call yourselves Christians are sent to render this service in the world. You must realize that perhaps the most important moment in the worship service is the moment in which you leave the church. Then it is decided whether you have understood why you spent that hour behind those walls. Do you realize that even when you are outside the walls of the church you nevertheless do not cease to be a congregation?

Your Christian service begins quite modestly with listening to the questions of men, talking them over, and holding your peace. They all have questions: the neighbor and the colleague at work, the head of a firm and the employee, the merchant, the public official, the farmer, the union official and the politician, the Marxist and the atheist. Whether or not they address their questions to *us* depends upon whether we take them seriously with *their* problems or whether we merely push our own questions and answers in front of us like a bulldozer that levels everything to "Christian" dimensions. We should allow their questions to confront us, and listen attentively to them. Our answers must have a solid foundation and must never be proposed on the basis of presumption or superficial views. The New Testament admonishes us: "Always be ready to give an answer to anyone who asks you concerning the ground of the hope that is in you" (I Peter 3:15).

Do we have a foundation and a hope that the others do not know? Can we give an account of the basis of this hope? Or do we all blow the same horn: "Men are bad; one is the other's devil; they make life difficult for each other; they are unable to live together either in small groups or as nations"? If we sing only this old song, then we have grasped nothing of the mighty acts of God by which he has made a new beginning between himself and us, between man and man, and also among the peoples of the earth. If we don't become involved in this God-established beginning, extending it between enemies and competitors, employers and employees, East and West, if we do not reckon with the possibility of the new in our midst, then we too are men without hope who think in the old lifeless categories of men and whom it is really worthless to question because, in this case, nothing distinguishes us from the other resigned people. But if the ground of our hope has been established, and we have heard it again in our gatherings, and have at the same time allowed this

99

ground to be placed under our feet so that we really stand upon it, then we cannot be satisfied with citing the pastor or "the church" but must ourselves speak to the questions of men and answer in the name of him under whose blessing we have gone out from the gathering and dispersed into the world.

Simply put, this means that *you* are the pastors, the shepherds and counselors among men. The theologians can no longer do this alone. That would be asking too much from them. *You* are with men in their places of residence and work. *You* walk along the same path they do. *You* have the same struggles and joys they do. *You* are close to them. When our Lord wishes to speak to men in the world today, he does it through *your* mouths. When he wishes to look at them today, he does it through *your* eyes. When he wishes to listen to their questions and petitions, he does it through *your* ears. When he wants to help someone, he does not reach down from heaven through a hole in the clouds but he uses *your* hands to reach in. When he goes to men on this earth, he uses *your* feet. Thus, in a very personal sense, *you* are his instruments. He has made you shepherds of your colleagues and pastoral counselors in your circle of acquaintances. No theologian or anyone else can relieve you of this service. *You* are called to it.

Your service consists at first simply in taking the other man as seriously as God does. You must speak with him, and you may not break off the dialogue once it has gotten started even if you have not reached any accord. For God does not cease to speak with us foolish and uncomprehending people. You are charged not only to answer with your mouth, but also to assume responsibility for the others—your group, organization, and society—by remaining together with them even when things get difficult and you derive no personal advantage from it. In the Sermon on the Mount we are charged to go the second mile when someone asks us to go with him the first mile. Our Lord went this second mile with men. But let us not deceive ourselves: Gethsemane and

Golgotha lie along the second mile! Service to and for men costs no less than that! Here we come to the line that divides Christian service from all humanitarian roads to "human relations" and "moral rearmament." This is the way it looks when someone following Jesus approaches another and becomes his neighbor.

We must be on guard against trivializing this service in dispersion, as if it consisted of proving our own salvation, on the one hand, and of offering a little meditation and some hymns in a factory or railroad station or dance hall, on the other. To become a *neighbor* is more dangerous and can even be fatal! Christians know this from the way of their Lord, and if they use both sacraments, they are continually made aware of the fact that new life comes only through the death of the old. But this really happens, since Jesus Christ has risen. *He* is our hope. Therefore as Christians, as congregation, and as church we do not need to aim at success and self-preservation. We live only when we are ready to lose ourselves in service to the world, spending ourselves—unto death. Therefore, every attempt in the church to get around this and to have it more cheaply is a convulsion, a lapse into senility, the end of the church.

Now, how do things actually stand in our gathered life? Do we direct our life as a *gathered* congregation with a view to our life in *dispersion?* Certainly our gathering is concerned first of all with the dialogue *God* initiates with us. Without *his* address to us in our gathering we would not be able to carry on any dialogue with men in the dispersion: this is implicit in the two-stroke cycle of which we spoke earlier. But we must ask whether the style and manner in which we come together today in our congregations—the way we listen, pray, praise, and give thanks—are in fact directed toward service in the world. It could be that our gathering actually has nothing to do with the dispersion. It could be that we are living in an unholy lie, leading a double life of merely apparent holiness, one in the congregation and a completely different one at home and in our place of work or organization.

If the congregation is to be in a condition that will allow it to respond to the questions of the world and to continue in dialogue with it in its dispersion, then it must be incessantly trained to do this when it is gathered. If Christians are to be catalyzers of brotherliness and community, responsibility and sacrifice, in their daily life, then they must not only be *called* to do this but they must also *practice* it in their gathered life. The world ought to see that in your gatherings free men get along with one another in a new way, without fear and mistrust. They respect one another even when there are differences of opinion. They know no hierarchical ladder from which one can look down upon the others from the vantage point of the office rungs and title rungs which happen for the moment to be higher. In the gathered congregation we learn how to get along with one another in a manner worthy of human beings, seeing in every other person first the man, and not the superior or inferior, the competitor or the other point of view. Such a congregation would irritate the world, command its attention, and even allow it to take hope. The gathering of Christians can be this and can have this effect. But, my brothers and sisters, we must be very clear that many things in our gatherings will have to be changed in order to accomplish this. We must be able to speak together there and help one another to find the answer to the questions put to us. Your children already confront you with questions at home. Don't simply pass them on to the religious teacher. Your vocational colleagues also raise sharp and disagreeable questions. Don't just refer them to the minister. Be sure to make them your own concern. Bring them with you into our gathering, lay them on the table, and don't be satisfied until in our common listening to God's Word we have found an answer for the world too.

Here in the gathering we are preparing ourselves for the "priesthood of all believers" that must be lived in home and vocation, in family and organization. To be sure, we have written "the priesthood of all believers" on the banner of Protestantism. But then it was placed in a glass case as a piece of tradition that we trot out during Reformation Day celebrations and also during a *Kirchentag*. In practice we do not have it, however. Where does it become visible that *you* —as baptized members of the congregation who, according to the word from First Peter, are "the chosen people," "the royal priesthood, a people for his possession"—*"proclaim* the mighty acts of him who has called you out of darkness into his wonderful light" (I Peter 2:9)? This word is spoken to all of you, not only to the ministers and church officials. But how will you want to open your mouth in the dispersion if you have not previously practiced this in the gathering? How will you be able to take seriously the men *outside* the church doors if this doesn't happen *inside* too?

Gathering and dispersion, worship service of God inside the church and your service of God in the world outside, belong inseparably together. The one is not without the other. Therefore it is very important that we advance beyond the infancy stage of our Christian existence. The minister is not your ecclesiastical nursemaid, who is supposed to have moderately warmed bottles to hand to you in your gatherings. Outgrow your baby shoes; grow up into the mature manhood of Jesus Christ—that is the word of the apostle Paul. Create for yourselves forms of congregational life that help you grow in knowledge and in the ability to speak out. Naturally, this involves babbling and stammering at first. Better you do that among yourselves, in the "family" of the congregation, than before the world. Don't allow your ministers any peace about this when you return home from this *Kirchentag*. The congregations here in Bavaria are moving in the right direction in their confessional diaspora situation when they hold worship services and Bible classes across the land under the leadership of lay teachers and other members of the congregation. This is no emergency solution but a sign of an *evangelical* congregation that is growing toward maturity.

103

We must allow an interruption at this point, however. Why, then, do we have theologians? Will our ministers be left without work? By no means! They will be given a job they will be able to do and for which their studies will have equipped them: they will become your helpers. It is not for you to be the minister's helper, enabling him to perform his ecclesiastical duties, but the reverse: the minister will be your helper, enabling you to perform your shepherding and pastoral service in the world. Out there are people who have no shepherd and wait for one. You are among them in the clashes of opinion—you, not the theologian. Let him know the questions you bring with you from your organizations and places of work. You have to set these in front of him so that he can think them through with you in relation to the Bible, and also be in a position to bring in other members of the congregation who have similar problems or who can help in some way. For you are not questioned as private individuals but as members of your congregation. Thus, the other members must help you to find the answer. The reason this man or this woman has been released from other work to devote himself to theological studies is to enable him to draw upon the counsel of the Bible in a competent fashion and to call attention to its direction. Thus he can help the congregation prepare for and accomplish its service in the world. So much the better for us if we have many and good theologians. But it is a luxury for every congregation to have a theologian today. In East Germany, hundreds of pastorates are vacant because there are too few theologians there. In that situation it is obvious that the function of the theologian in the future can no longer be that of the sole minister and pastoral counselor. He will be much more the helper of the members of the congregation who will themselves perform the service of shepherds and pastoral counselors. That is the work of the theologian and that is what you must call upon him for.

Our thinking about theologians and nontheologians, ministers and members of the congregation, must be reversed.

That is not an easy thing to do. There are enough people in our church who doubt the validity of this view or who point to experiments that miscarried, generalize upon the aberrations of the sects or caricature this matter so as to make it laughable. But here at this *Kirchentag* all of you are asked—and I hope you will take this question back to your home congregations—whether what I have said to you corresponds to the New Testament. If you answer affirmatively, then you can no longer continue in your congregations as you did before. You must break new ground. You must not put up with any clerical directorship but begin to live as a member of your congregation who has come of age. The "world come of age," about which people speak today, needs as its counterpart, not the minister and the church officials, but a *congregation come of age!*

We theologians will also have to revise our thinking and become more modest. We will have to guard against being devoured by administrative matters and not allow ourselves to be misused as speakers for every sort of assembly and celebration. Indeed, we will train members of the congregation so that eventually they will be able to take over responsibility for the so-called acts of the pastoral office. We need not worry if failures occur or if things are said badly or mistakes are made in the first attempts. A mother is happy for every word her child utters, no matter how garbled, simply because the child is trying to speak. We must begin that modestly with our congregations, too, because despite four hundred years of Protestantism, we haven't gotten any farther than that. The Reformation has remained bogged down at this point! It must go farther if we do not want to lose it entirely. The Evangelical Church is *ecclesia semper reformanda*—a church in which reformation never ceases.

Thank God this is not merely the music of the distant future. Such things already happen in our midst. Often they remain concealed. Sometimes they are but timidly practiced, although church laws and regulations already encourage them.

105

Sometimes congregations and groups must defend themselves against the accusation of fanaticism and betrayal to the world. But this happens. Sometimes it is a local congregation that has learned to understand itself and its commission in a new way. I think, for example, of one that took its life together so earnestly that it turned the announcement period during the worship service into a conversation between the members of the congregation concerning the tasks coming up that week. Sometimes these discussions lasted longer than the minister's sermon. There are already congregations in which the members meet together with the minister before Sunday in order to work with him on the sermon for Sunday and who have also begun to have something to say in the worship service itself. Happily there are also house circles in existence here and there in our country. They sit down together for independent Bible study and call upon the theologian only when they need his specialized knowledge. In addition, we should open our eyes and learn from other churches, those in Africa and Asia too. A few weeks ago I had the experience of worshiping with the Evangelical Christians (Baptists) in Moscow and Leningrad. Two thousand and five hundred men engaged in corporate worship. The elders prayed and read the Scriptures, ministers preached, and all gave answers to questions that were raised. They stood crowded together. Some sang from hymnbooks they had written themselves, and many wrote down the sermon in order to tell it to others in the family and in the neighborhood or to send it in letters to all parts of the country. One sensed that this congregation was composed entirely of veritable shepherds and pastoral counselors, and that the grandmothers as well as the young workers all knew about their commission in the congregation and in the world. The body of Jesus Christ is always larger, more extensive, more comprehensive and richer in the variety of its members than our ecclesiastical organization and its traditional partitioning of offices.

From the work of the Gossner Mission in the East and in the West, in which I am involved, I know of other examples of congregations of men from industry in whose midst preaching and speaking occurs in an unconventional manner, often without pulpit or altar, but always with the Bible and the Sacrament at the center. When baptisms are held, the gathered congregation discusses the meaning of baptism and its practical consequences with the parents and sponsors. For the Lord's Supper, we sit at the same table that is otherwise set for our daily meals. Before we pass the bread and the wine to each other we talk with one another about what happened at the first Lord's Supper table. At weddings the father of the bride reads the text or prays with his house congregation. At burials, friends and those close to the bereaved family testify what they as a congregation have learned and believed from the Bible in view of death.

Another example: Can an industrial congregation celebrate Thanksgiving Day in the same way as a rural congregation? Perhaps it will express its thanks the way that industrial congregation in England did which did not celebrate the day as a harvest festival, the traditional significance of the day, but, rather, as a day of thanks for industry. The engineer placed a steel bar on the altar; the miner, a piece of coal; and the woman textile worker, a roll of cloth. In that way they expressed their thanks for the preservation of their place of work and thereby also for the preservation of their families. If the congregation really loves men, it must do everything it can to enable its forms of worship to be understood. Where it does that, members of organizations, corporations and trade unions, political parties and other groups, come out even today and start the conversation with Christians, and want to know what they think about the way the world is going and about men and their life together. Do they meet a congregation that knows what it has to do in the world? The decisive thing is that we avoid regarding our congregation as an end in itself and look upon it instead as the instrument of God, with whose help he wills to make all men into his people. Let it be repeated once again: the congregation of Jesus Christ exists in a twofold way, always in both together, as gathered

107

around the Word and Sacrament, *and* as dispersed in the world. Its life is similar to the inhaling and exhaling of one and the same body. Neither the one nor the other can be omitted if one wants to live. It is exactly this way with the congregation.

We have come to the close. Our theme has been: "Congregation Without Walls." At which points can we still erect a wall *in* the congregation, *around* the congregation, or *outside* the congregation? The answer is, Nowhere, for if we do that, we cease to be a congregation. Nowhere may we seek security for ourselves; nowhere may we hide ourselves. God fetches us out and brings us to the place he wants us to be: in the world in service to the men he loves. Our God has a passion for men that goes so far that he really suffers with them and for them. He allows us to share in this passion—and in this suffering. He wills that no bad experiences with men (he indeed made them) should turn us away from them. He sends us out to infect men with this passion so that they will also become his co-workers. We should be contagiously human. He incorporates us into the congregation to make us capable of being so. His congregation is no reservation for religiously inclined people, surrounded by walls and regarded by the world with either a friendly or a critically tolerant attitude. Rather, it is the port of reshipment at which God's supply is taken in and immediately passed on to the world. Therefore, we all have our hands full and have no time to devote to the construction of church walls.

Where we nevertheless continue to raise them, God will tear them down as he has always done in the past, indeed, often with the help of the heathen. Where the world forces the congregation into a ghetto, however, there we will not want to tarry long with complaints and accusations, but instead joyfully confess with the Bible: "By my God I can leap over a wall" (Ps. 18:29).

108

PART III. THE SERVICE OF CHRISTIANS IN THE INDUSTRIAL WORLD

7

THE SERVICE OF CHRISTIANS
TO MAN IN THE SECULAR WORLD

"SERVICE is a part of adoration of God and witnesses to his love for us and all men." (Report of the Section on Service of the Third Assembly of the World Council of Churches, held in New Delhi, 1961; par. 3.) Especially in relation to the secular man, witness to the love of God will have to take the form of service. Service is a sign of what Jesus did for the world and at the same time a report about the way he exercises his Lordship without compulsion in self-giving love. "As the Father sent him, so he sends us to sacrifice ourselves in his service." (*Ibid.*) God sends us into the world, and today that means the secular world.

By "secular" we mean that man makes his decisions in the realms of thought and action on his own responsibility. He claims and demonstrates the possibility of ordering the world on the basis of intraworldly perspectives. He rejects tutelage by some higher being of the sort variously named and described by religions. Christianity shared in setting this development in motion. Furthermore, Christianity should continue to affirm it because it represents a farther step toward man's assumption of responsibility for shaping the world and his corporate life. In this way it corresponds to the commission of God, who calls man to responsibility and will not allow him to pass off responsibility for the course of history onto religious powers.

In this paper we shall investigate three things:

I. How witness can be accomplished in the form of service by Christians dispersed throughout the structures of society.

II. The significance of the gathered congregation for the witness of its dispersed members in the secular world.

III. At what point the service of the theologian has to be introduced into the gathered as well as the dispersed life of the congregation.

I. THE SERVICE OF THE CHRISTIAN IN THE STRUCTURES OF SOCIETY

1. The Christian is simultaneously a member of his congregation and of the secular world. Conscious identification with this secular world is neither necessary nor possible, since as a citizen, as one pursuing his vocation, as a member of an organization, even as father, mother, or child, he *is* already inevitably a man of his time and of his world. He cannot be a Christian apart from his status in these other respects from one moment to another. On the contrary, he must constantly ask himself whether and in what way he can actually be a Christian while holding one or another such status. Therefore it will be impossible for him to be indifferent about the manner of his activity. His choice of vocation will not be determined solely by the question of money and opportunity for advancement, but, rather, by the question whether this work offers the possibility of serving other men as a servant of Jesus Christ. Such a consideration will also determine his decisions about which organizations in society he will take part in and which he will refuse. If he has no choice in this matter—and this is very often the case in our time—he will nevertheless attempt to perform this service even under the most adverse conditions. If he is hindered in this, or his service is without results, he will understand this not as something that exempts him from this service but as participation in Christ's suffering. This means that for Christians there is in the last analysis no situation that can prevent their service

as disciples of Jesus Christ. For just as the suffering and dying of their Lord was the distinctive sign of his unreserved service to the world, so in the case of Christians, too, suffering and dying are the signs of their service to the world.

2. Christian service in the contemporary world must not be limited to neighbor love on the part of individuals. It must be effective today in the associations and *organizations* that determine the direction of socioeconomic development. A few examples of such service may be listed:

—keeping organizations open to change and in motion;

—standing alongside those who work within them and protecting them against manipulation and violations of human dignity, because Jesus Christ preferred to be despised himself rather than to allow another to be treated with contempt;

—discarding outmoded taboos; raising questions, even uncomfortable ones; unmasking intransigent insistence upon the *status quo* and its (perhaps religious) rationalizations as sinful bondage to the "old age";

—considering the possibility of a new beginning, and helping to create the stabilizing nuclei of a new social reality;

—refusing to regard as final any enmity between men or between their groups and organizations;

—breaking down walls of division between races, peoples, religions, and ideologies, because Jesus Christ set himself to demolishing the walls of hostility between men which also separate us from God (Eph. 2:14).

3. Involvement in organizations often means that the Christian comes to share a group interest which stands in competition with the interests of other groups. He will therefore have

113

to be careful, on the one hand, never to represent the interest of his group as the ultimate goal for all but advocate it only to the extent that it does not harm or defraud the brother in the other group. He will have to strive to keep his group from making any totalitarian claims. Participation in the gathered life of the church should help him maintain the necessary critical distance from his group. On the other hand, the Christian will welcome the opportunity to work together with other men in a social group when it is content to pursue partial goals and refrain from ideological propagandizing for totalitarian goals for mankind. It is part of Christian humility to be content with such partial tasks, and to expect that a viable social order for all men will be worked out through the efforts of the various groups and organizations in society. Naturally, he will insist that every effort be made to bring about worldwide unification of the peoples of the earth, provided such efforts are aimed at peace for all. The Christian is like a hound who thrusts his nose to the earth, trying to keep on the track of his Lord in order to find him at work in the secular world.

4. Such service is at the same time a witness to the freedom God gives to his children. Wherever the Christian finds tendencies toward such a service in the world he will join hands with it. He knows that Jesus Christ is the Lord of the world and that he works in it in a thousand different ways with the most diverse kinds of men. Wherever men take responsibility for their fellowmen; wherever men love each other, and bear one another's burdens and disappointments; wherever they are ready to suffer for one another—there Jesus Christ *is* already at work. Wherever we discover his work in the midst of secular endeavors we are called to share in it.

As a result of their involvement in service to individual men and their assumption of responsibility for social organizations, Christians may find themselves both permitted and required to make a verbal witness to Jesus Christ under certain circumstances. But they do not possess any ready-made supply of fixed formulations or clichés for such occasions.

Indeed, they ought not to insert any prefabricated witness into the secular situation. For they have the promise that they will be given the power to bear the appropriate witness to the name of the Lord whenever they are confronted with such situations.

II. THE SIGNIFICANCE OF THE GATHERED CONGREGATION FOR THE SERVICE OF CHRISTIANS IN THE SECULAR WORLD

The idea has increasingly come to the fore in ecumenical conversations that the action of the gathered congregation must be oriented toward the life and witness of its members in the world. When the congregation gathers, it does not emigrate from the secular world. No other reality surrounds the congregation and no other theme motivates it when it is gathered than that of the Servanthood-Lordship of Jesus Christ in the secular world. The gathered congregation is a servant witness to this just as much as the dispersed congregation.

In contrast to the service of the dispersed members of the congregation living and working in the secular world, the "gathered congregation" stands not only for worship services, groups, and circles meeting in churches but also for all the ecclesiastical institutions, offices, organs, and agencies that the congregation has created for itself.

1. Congregational worship is a matter of adoration, petition, and intercession, and—as "hearing" and "speaking" under the Biblical Word—it is a conversation of Christian witnesses with one another and with the Biblical witnesses. The subject of this conversation cannot properly be determined simply by means of ecclesiastical norms that have been handed down through history. The experience and practice that the witnesses have had in the world must also be taken into account. It is not the task of worship simply to read and clarify the Biblical Word without reference to the reality of life. Rather, the reality of life in the world is precisely what needs to be clarified by referring it to the Biblical Word. In this way the

worship services and various group meetings in the churches would actually equip the members for service in the secular world. This view implies that the language of the worship service must be suitable for witness in the secular world (cf. I Cor. 14:6–19)—to name only one consequence of this. Christians are moved by the experiences they have with their Lord in the world to gather together to talk about them, give corporate thanks for them, and in prayer and in conversation with the Biblical witnesses allow themselves to be given new direction, new hope, and new courage.

2. While it is true that the congregation does not emigrate from the world when it gathers together, nevertheless it does place itself at a distance from all the ties that characterize the secular world (Gal. 3:28). Admittedly, it is not allowed to remain permanently in this position of distance, as if it were some sort of "perfect society." It must again and again disperse into the secular world.

In this dispersion the individual Christian has no other way to be a witness than within these worldly ties—as worker or employer, as a member of Eastern or Western civilization. Where his responsibility demands it and his conscience permits him, he may voluntarily engage in political action groups and various interest groups within the social order, despite the particularism always connected with such groups. No special, conscious act of identification with secular society is necessary before the Christian can become engaged in such groups, however. The Christian witness is always already a member of secular society, as we have seen.

On the other hand, the gathered congregation, including its organization, administration, and leaders, may not under any circumstances identify itself with secular society. It may never bind itself so as to become "the church of the state," or the church of this or that people, the church of the West, of the whites or the blacks, or the church of the working classes. It must never allow itself to understand itself this way or to shape itself along such lines. History and tradition burden many churches with ties of this sort. They are outmoded. Christians cannot and may not accept, either for themselves or for others, offers of special privileges for some religion or confession that the state or some social institution wants to grant. This sort of guarantee for its witness renders it unworthy of belief. Christians should instead stand for religious freedom in their country. Through their service in the structures of the secular world they should fight for the rights of men of all persuasions, also atheists, to live according to their convictions.

3. In contrast to this, it should also be said that the gathered congregation can and should make use of structural patterns of secular society in developing its own order. The church, too, must be organized and administered. It possesses no special "holy," unchangeable order binding it to traditional forms and archaic practices.

No simple imitation of the world is implied here, however. Just as the dispersed congregation is a witness to its Lord and in this way becomes "the salt of the earth," so the gathered congregation in all that it comprises—forms of fellowship, organization, administration, leadership, with corporate worship the center of it all—must also be a witness to its Lord and thus "a city set on a hill." The gathered congregation has a very important task precisely at this point. The secular society in which it lives is learning today that the most important decisions for men's social life are no longer the decisions they reach as individuals but, rather, those which are the result of common efforts. In the most varied ways and on the basis of the most diverse presuppositions, society is struggling today to fulfill its historical task in national and international life. This task is to find the step from "I" to "we" in a way that provides for the respect due the person in society.

The Christian congregation as a gathering of persons has always aimed at this. It cannot, of course, relieve secular society of this task, but it can provide a kind of exemplary service. Its forms of fellowship and organization provide an exceptionally advantageous practice field in which people may learn how to live and speak together, celebrate and have a good time together. Here they may learn how young and old, men and women, black and white, rich and poor, can get along with each other and establish a community; how to build bridges and overcome misunderstandings; how the individual can fit himself into a larger whole and at the same time preserve his dignity; how one organizes and administers without becoming lifeless and inhuman; how one leads or allows himself to be led without becoming unbrotherly or falling prey to the enticements of power or of being a subordinate.

To be sure, church practice is often the opposite of this kind of exemplary social life. Instead, worldly patterns of human relationships are simply taken over on the grounds that "unfortunately, it won't work any other way." In doing this the church appropriates uncritically false lines of development often after secular society has already abandoned them. It is a bad omen that in the administration of the church in Germany all the "vertical" relationships (e.g., of authorization and execution) function rather well, whereas all horizontal forms of cooperation (e.g., working together as colleagues; teamwork; collective initiative without initiation "from above") function rather badly or not at all (cf. Matt. 25:25 ff.). It is also a bad omen when many churches are nearly a century behind secular society in their attitude toward women. In the formation of interpersonal relationships and the patterns of community life, the church not only should but *must* be progressive. It must always be ready to go a step farther and to take risks. It owes the world this exemplary service if it is to accomplish its witness.

4. This insight regarding the church's responsibility for exemplary progressiveness broke through very early at one point in the church's life, namely, in the area of charity. Long before the consciousness of social responsibility had become widespread in secular society, Christians and Christian

churches took the initiative in developing accommodations and organizations for the care of the poor, the sick, the helpless, and for children. The Christian community set up models of social responsibility by establishing hospitals, homes, orphanages, and nursing orders.

The service of these exemplary models has borne fruit at many points. Society recognized its responsibility and sought to fulfill it through a variety of governmental, communal, and private institutions and arrangements. But needs always arise that the established welfare institutions cannot meet, such as the need for psychological help or the loneliness of the aged. At these points the members of the Christian community are personally called to step into the breach today just as they did in the past.

Wherever society has taken up this sort of social responsibility the Christian community can address itself to new tasks. New Delhi reminded us again that the primary form of the social diaconate of Christianity today does not have to be the same everywhere in the world, nor must it necessarily be that of charitable care. Wherever society has learned to take care of the sick and the helpless, Christians can and should perform this sort of service within the secular institutions just as they would offer their service in other secular jobs. No new Christian hospitals need to be built under such circumstances. Other social models will be needed, however, to provide some new impulse for society. For this reason, it is sound and sensible for Christian congregations to take the initiative in setting up cooperative farms and apprenticeship shops in lands undergoing rapid social transformation. Yet even these models will be superfluous one day after their purpose of providing an initial impulse has been accomplished. The meaning of all churchly diaconal establishments is not to set up a "Christian society" alongside the worldly social order so that Christians may dwell happily among themselves divorced from the world, but, rather, to help the secular society to find its way to more human relationships and forms of organization.

119

III. WHERE THE SERVICE OF THE THEOLOGIAN COMES IN

There are many definitions of a "theologian." We are speaking of theology in the sense of an academic, scientific discipline of the sort that has been given rather exalted significance in the congregational life of many European and American churches by virtue of the fact that most of their professional office bearers have taken an academic course of theological studies.

1. As a rule, the calling of an academic theologian leads to some ecclesiastical office. Thus, the theologian stands in the midst of the gathered congregation. His work often goes on without consideration of the actual experiences and existential problems of secular men. For this reason, it is imperative that things such as the socioeconomic determination of modern life, the "bodiliness" (materiality) and the autonomy of secular life, be taken seriously throughout the course of his theological education, so that he may learn to love the fullness of secular life and learn to discern the Lordship of Christ over this broad horizon. The theologian will have to be careful not to lose his critical distance in the midst of his dialogue with the secular world. If that happened, he would alienate himself from the message he is commissioned to bear and would also subject the message to evanescent criteria.

2. Witness to men in the secular world demands not only the service of the scattered laity living within it. It demands also the direct confrontation of theologians with the social order. This can be brought about in several ways.

a. The theologian in the office of the local pastor should be given the opportunity to participate for a limited period of time in the secular decisions that are made in economics, politics, culture, and science.

b. Where the entire churchly and congregational life depends on the activity and initiative of the professional theologian (pastor), the monologue of the pastor with himself should be displaced by dialogue with the laity in order that secular experience may get a hearing in the congregation. Only if this happens can the pastor's flock of listeners become a service group of witnesses to Jesus Christ in the secular world.

c. Theologians should be released or, rather, called in increasing numbers to extracongregational work, so that dialogue with organizations and unions can be better observed.

d. There should also be an increasing number of theologians whose vocational position should be in the midst of contemporary society as workers or salaried employees, parliamentarians or journalists, etc., so that they will experience in concrete form what it means to bear responsibility for secular life. Forms of authorization and cooperation must be found that will make the experiences and insights of such theologians fruitful for the life of the Christian community.

Theologians in extracongregational service and in other vocations should pay attention to realities more perceptively and patiently than theologians in pastoral offices or in academic teaching positions are able to do. They should learn vicariously for the parish-bound theologians what possibilities and dangers, which forms of suffering and hope, sympathy, help, alienation, destruction, reconciliation and healing, preoccupy and affect men in the secular world. They should discover which changes are in progress in society; which are necessary and which are threatening. They should uncover the theological relevance of the most concrete social facts and processes of the sort that can be grasped only by having lived through them with others, deliberated together about them and come to common decisions. Some examples of these facts and processes would be: the advancement standards of industrial society; the subtle processes regulating power, justice, and order in a pluralism of interest groups and powers of influence; changes in the structures and functions of property; the positive and negative effects of the anonymization and impersonalization of certain human relationships; the new forms of authority and subordination.

121

Theologians with such experience could help the churches get over the superficial cultural pessimism of some theological or supposedly theological schools of thought. They would discover for the churches what things in the secular world are "true, honorable, just, pure, lovely, gracious, excellent, praiseworthy," and help them to "think about" these things (Phil. 4:8 f.). They would help us "prove what is the will of God, what is good and acceptable and perfect" (Rom. 12:2).

If theologians would experience how much effort, self-lessness, renunciation, love, readiness to assume responsibility and to step in to help a fellowman, etc., actually goes on within the structures and relationships of modern secularized society, then they would also have opened up to them the diaconal meaning of their own ministry. There are individuals and groups in positions of social responsibility in the secular world who treasure dialogue with theologians because they are concerned to discover the broader horizons and deeper dimensions of the problems and decisions with which they are dealing. To this end the theologian in a position of secular responsibility can make a decisive contribution.

The witness that Jesus Christ is risen and is the Lord of the world must confront secular men in our time in the form of sacrificial service for their sake. This happens when Christians in their work and in their social involvements reckon with the reality of the new world in the midst of the old. If they think, speak, and act only in the schema of the old world, no one will believe their message about the resurrection. If they act in reliance upon the superiority of forgiveness, brotherliness, and peace, they will certainly appear to many as fools, purveyors of fantasies, illusions, and nonsense. They know, however, that since the first Easter this new world of God's has been a reality and not only a hope. That is why they are ready even to allow themselves to be laughed at and perhaps thrown out of the company of their fellowmen. The cross appears wherever the reality of the resurrection is seriously reckoned with among men today. They always belong together.

8

PASTORAL CARE IN INDUSTRIAL PLANTS
—POSSIBILITIES AND LIMITS

"Pastoral care in the plant" is a terrible phrase. It recalls the
Works Welfare Department and the plant kindergarten, which,
of course, are useful and good institutions. Should an industrial chaplain now step alongside the personnel manager, psy-
chologist, welfare officer, and the plant doctor? To this, the
answer must be, "No." That would be to act as though the
employees of a plant were our objects, which we had to
"treat." Those taking part in our six-month Seminar for the
Church's Service in Industrial Society all reported that they
were not the givers and distributors during the time of their
industrial work, but quite the contrary. Their fellow workers
were the ones who gave them trust, comradeship, and help as
a matter of course.

I. Machines Confront Man

The participants in our seminar, who were all theologians,
first of all found themselves for once the object of the factory
system and of men. They experienced the claims that the
changing shifts make upon both spirit and body. They understood that suddenly they were no longer confronted with men
but with machines—machines that they could not stop and
whose speed and tempo set the pace for them. They grasped
why the plant was a world of its own which a man readily
forsook the moment the buzzer went off so that he could get

on with what is supposedly "real living." They noticed that they were kept ten hours a day, travel time included, in a world of work whose worth was expressed solely in terms of money on payday.

II. THE STARTING POINT: CARE OF ONE'S OWN SOUL

Of what significance is it, for example, that a married woman sees nothing of her husband at his work, and vice versa? A woman can hardly interest herself in what her husband does in his hours of work. Her chief concern must be his rate of pay. What a burden is placed upon the marriage partners by the fact that they are partners only during free time and sleep but not at work! By contrast, a man works with a completely different woman while he is on the job, often having more conversation with her than he has with his wife during his leisure time when he is tired. What must pastoral care look like under such circumstances for a man and wife to whom we have said, perhaps only a short time ago at the altar, that God made woman to be a helpmate for man—but not in the sense of a woman other than the wife becoming the helper of a strange man at work.

What becomes of my Sunday if I am busy in a continuously operating factory? One can go on like this with numberless examples. But the small points that have been made ought to suffice to make clear that pastoral work in the modern industrial world begins with the care of one's own soul.

III. TAKING THE OTHERS SERIOUSLY

The experiences of other men and organizations cannot relieve the pastor today of the responsibility of taking the step that leads him into the midst of men in the plants and into the midst of their problems. All pastoral care rests upon the presupposition that I love the others whom I want to help. "Thou shalt love thy neighbor as thyself" is the only basis upon which all pastoral work can be carried out. "To love" means, after all, somewhat modestly expressed to be sure, to take the other seriously. And the other wants to be taken seriously precisely at those places in his life at which he rubs himself raw. There are many such places in the plant. For this reason it is insufficient to know merely a man's domestic circumstances. In early times (and even yet in the country) it was taken for granted that the pastor knew about the worries and joys of his peasants. He could understand immediately how a village family could be left destitute after a hailstorm, for he had in some measure experienced the catastrophe himself among the apple trees in the vicarage garden. He most certainly dealt with this event in his conversations and perhaps also in his Sunday sermon. But where does the man engaged in industrial work find an echo and an answer to his needs? Here we are in a most difficult position. Neither the residential neighborhood nor industry constitutes an integrated whole. The situation in the village and in the small town was quite different. There were common interests in them, even if they consisted of nothing more than the common hope for good harvest weather. Our world of work is so specialized and broken up that there may well be no one who can comprehend even as little as one sector of it. Even the management of an industrial works is composed of specialists who are knowledgeable only in the areas actually assigned to them.

IV. FAREWELL TO THE CLERGY'S MONOPOLY OF PASTORAL WORK

How can one person—be he the minister, a friend, or one's own wife—understand the problems, needs, and temptations of another and be of help to him? Certainly a single individual can no longer do this. A team must step into his place, composed of men who expect something from Jesus Christ for their life, something not only for their personal and private existence but also for their professional tasks and their place of work. If they have fellowship with one another and yet remain oriented toward other men, then at any given time the appropriate pastor for this particular man or this particular situation can emerge from their own midst. All this means, to be sure,

125

bidding good-by to the spiritual monopoly of the clergy. Such a monopoly did exist and still does exist in practice in the Evangelical Church, but it cannot claim Biblical authority. In the sort of "pastoral team" that has been outlined, the theologically trained man can be a good helper. But he can no longer solve the questions raised in a plant or by industrial society generally. In the light of what has already been said, it will be clear that help for men in the plant is not a matter of providing religious conversations or of making a pronouncement of general Christian doctrines. It is much more a matter of help in a concrete situation. Very often a worker feels himself to be in the wrong place; another feels his work has not been given due recognition; a third considers himself misunderstood or suppressed by a superior; a fourth seems to be unable to work together with the particular fellow worker with whom he has been teamed up.

V. Supporting the Informal Groups in the Plant

In preliminary discussions of this article with white-collar and blue-collar workers from three plants, many examples were brought forward from life in the plant. All those who took part declared unanimously that it was unlikely that a minister could help in the solution of these problems if he did not leave his ministerial dignity and authority behind him upon going through the factory gate. A few had already experienced help in such situations, however, from a fellow worker or a superior, to be sure. In all plants, cutting across and overlapping with the formal work groups, there are so-called informal groups, i.e., groups that hold together in a special way. Sometimes an extramural common interest, sometimes simply congeniality and friendship, form the basis of such completely unplanned and unorganized groups. These groups are what humanize the machine world of industry, or at least make it bearable. That is why precisely such groups which one finds already present in the plant can be used as the starting point of pastoral work in the plant. Such pastoral work does not have to be created *ex nihilo*. These informal groups carry out such service already in a completely unconscious and unintentional way. One ought to strengthen them as much as possible. Conflict often arises at the place where the necessary demands of the plant clash with the equally necessary resistance of conscience in situations in which technical and economic requirements threaten to roll over the needs of the men as men. Superiors—from foremen to the chairman of the board—often find themselves in discord when the question arises: "Is man more important than production?"

VI. Ministers Must Be Free Men

Thus a clarification in genuine matters of conscience is needed precisely by the responsible officials of a plant. Whether or not this is ever expected and sought is another question.

In the last analysis, only a man who has an indestructible hope for man, and for whom there is no such thing as a hopeless case, can be called a pastor. To practice this hope in a plant—both at the top level and the bottom level—requires a freedom that will not be shattered again and again by fear of other men. For this reason, the person engaged in pastoral care must be a free man. But is this not utopian? Perhaps hope and freedom are still possible with respect to a single man. But are they still possible with respect to the technical system of a plant, economic laws, and, finally, with respect to the organization, whether it be that of the employers or that of the employees? How many gods of this kind are there in our society, and especially in the plants that inexorably demand our service? Profits, bureaucracy, organization—these seem to be the modern principalities and powers that are not of flesh and blood but with which we must struggle, as Paul wrote. The individual finds himself helpless with respect to these powers and therefore needs his colleagues and friends. Here again, only the informal group (or whatever one chooses to call this quiet understanding among the men that runs right through the whole hierarchy of the plant) can help.

127

VII. The Goal Is the Alteration of the System for Man

One must probably fight against these anonymous powers and gods of our technical and economic system which desire man's unconditional subjection. But this is hard and risky because man receives his daily bread from these very forces. Precisely at this point, however, pastoral care is a confession to man. And is it not at the same time thereby a confession to that God who risked himself for the sake of man? It is an error to expect from pastoral work in the plant mere pacification and the improvement of the atmosphere of the plant. For the object of pastoral care is not the improvement of production but the humanization of organized work, and also, for just this reason, the alteration of a system that makes men mere cogs in the technological and economic apparatus. The *limits* of pastoral care in industry for the church and its commissioned ministers we have seen. The *tasks* of pastoral care in the plant are greater and more manifold than it was possible to indicate here. The *possibilities* of industrial pastoral work lie in this, that Christians in the factories will not emigrate secretly with their beliefs but will witness to them where they are by the fact that, like their Lord, they are always "for" other people or their fellowship. Then they will continually come back again to the point at which they need the renewal of their commission and encouragement for their daily service to their neighbor.

Now they themselves need pastoral care. The whole church will be responsible for seeing that they are not left alone. The fact that then pastors (literally, "shepherds"), too, will seek and find their way to the flock in the plant is already an experience for which both church members and the men in the plant can be equally thankful.

9

THESES ON CODETERMINATION
IN THE WORK PROCESS

> *Modern industrial society has
> not yet arrived at a normal
> condition, and the search for
> this pulsates through our en-
> tire social life.*
> —Friedrich Naumann.

I. THE SOCIAL QUESTION

1. The overwhelming majority of employees are involved in
a process of work structured along authoritarian lines, in
which nothing more is expected of them than conscientious,
diligent, and disciplined adherence to received instructions.
The basic problem of the contemporary world of work is the
fact that the employee is placed under the tutelage of a
production organization which gives him the role of one who
simply receives commands, since those in charge expect
nothing from their subordinates but conscientious, diligent,
and disciplined adherence to received instructions, thereby
depriving him of his status as a mature human being.

2. Man can actualize his humanity only in the sort of work
that allows him to be an acting subject, not a mere object that
is acted upon; that enables him to be a person of the same

value as any other person. Even in the world of work, responsible cooperation (*Mitarbeit*, literally, "working together") belongs to the essence of human existence.

Responsible cooperation means more than simply working under a sense of duty. Responsible cooperation occurs only when the employee has a part in the formation, organization, and evaluation of his work; when he can speak, act, and decide on these matters together with his superiors and fellow employees.

Prof. A. Rich: "The dehumanizing segregation of the worker as a responsible person out of the industrial work process, and his dehumanizing integration into this process as an 'instrumental work force,' signifies essentially what the fate of man is in the modern production organization."

3. It will not do to urge men in the direction of leisure, family life, and political activities, with explanations that there they will find ample opportunity to be human. Man is decisively influenced and molded by his vocational work. If he is shorn of mature responsibility in his vocational life and merely used as an "instrumental work force," he is dehumanized.

Prof. A. Rich: "Whoever feels cheated of his personal dignity, responsible life, and genuine human fellowship in the world of work will feel cheated of these things generally—even if he lives in a politically free democracy."

4. The plant is the place from which the social, vocational, and economic destiny of the worker emanates. His social freedom or unfreedom begins there. There the larger social order becomes visible and meaningful to him in practical terms. Can it realistically be expected that a man who in his plant is compelled to be a passive object and recipient of commands will be able to be a responsible citizen who actively supports and shapes a democratic society along with his fellow citizens?

De Tocqueville: "It is really difficult to see how men who have completely renounced the custom of ruling themselves will be in a position to make sound choices of those who are to rule over them; and it will not be possible to make anyone believe that a freedom-loving, vigorous, and wise government can ever proceed from the votes of a slave people."

II. Halfway Measures

5. The heart of the social problem today, which is characterized by the fact that there are men in the industrial enterprise who in their work are mere "numbers," will not be solved either by good wages or by reasonable treatment of the commodity "work force."

This problem will persist despite codetermination at the top level of plants and companies, indeed, even if there should be socialization of the means of production.

6. The principles of modern leadership in the plant that are being propagated and practiced today do not go beyond the concept of manipulating the employees. They take certain human tendencies into consideration, to be sure, but they do not do justice to the genuinely human. Manipulation is refined, but it does not become more social because essential factors are lacking. Constant exchange of views and mutual cooperation with the co-workers does not occur, nor do the co-workers have the opportunity to exercise a continual influence upon the decision-making processes in the plant.

7. The codetermination provided by well-known institutions such as the Plant Workers Council, the Director of Work, and the Employees Supervisory Board has given the employees the opportunity of influencing the decisions of the employers and managers.

Codetermination anchored in law respects the maturity of the employee class, but it does not decisively alter the social status of the individual worker.

Transposition of structures from the political realm to the plant will not do justice to the necessities of industrial production because necessities that obtain in the plant are different from those to be found in the state.

8. The employee is taken more seriously today by companies and plants than he used to be. His situation, point of view,

and wishes are taken into consideration. But management thinks for the employee, and the employee remains a passive, manipulated object. The industrial work force will become a subject, a human being, only when he too, the worker, may speak, converse with, and express himself to those in charge.

III. THE TASK

9. A felt contradiction in social prestige, whether in society generally or in the plant, must eventually lead to severe conflicts. The mature employee cannot be separated from his place in social life, and both demand recognition in his work as well.

10. The present status of the employee is not an automatic result of technological development. On the contrary! Conditions in production technology, which are characterized by ever more advanced division of labor, automation, and the pressure of optimal profitability, demand responsible cooperative participation of all the co-workers, including those who are not the "leading co-workers" (i.e., foremen, etc.).

It is noteworthy that one successful American businessman sees his only chance of gaining an advantage over his competition in the drawing out and activating of the latent abilities and gifts of the workers themselves.

Technical development is pressing toward a system of work that releases spontaneous activity, and it will succeed in this development against all the resistance of those groups who have thus far held privileged positions in the plants.

11. The present state of developments in production technology as well as the educational level and state of mind of the workers call for a system of work that allows the individual employee to engage in responsible cooperation and thereby makes possible codetermination in the process of work.

12. The incorporation of employees into the work process as responsible persons does not mean the surrender of the strict order necessary for the operation of a plant. No company could

get along without dividing the totality of workers into those who lead and those who are led. A smoothly operating flow of production demands the construction of a purposeful order with different levels of function and responsibility.

It would be sensible to build into this order institutions that would make possible real rights of consultation and codetermination for the employees. The decisive point here is that the employee be given this right in the area in which he is most qualified and competent, namely, in his own place of work, department, and working group.

Prof. A. Rich: "The employee will be able to have a voice in his work and thereby become a man who can understand himself as a subject in the process of production only if his initiative, resourcefulness, and zest for enterprise is consciously sought, demanded, and honored in the production process."

IV. WHAT REMAINS TO BE DONE

13. As an example of one such institution we cite the committees of specialists in which common deliberations aimed at making decisions for the entire company are carried on between those in charge of the planning in various departments and the elected delegates from among the co-workers who are involved in the actual production work.

14. Alongside these already familiar committees of specialists, consultations should be set up at the place of work as the necessary presupposition for every single worker having the opportunity to participate in the process of deliberating and deciding upon every issue that comes up for debate with respect to him and his working group.

15. These consultations on work at the level of the working groups and at the departmental level should be incorporated into the plant organization, taking the following things into consideration:

In order to allow these consultations on the work process really to become the affair of the workers themselves, they should:

133

a. Be made responsible to the Plant Council in order to guarantee that they are conducted in an orderly manner.

b. Their preparation should be in the hands of the authorized union shop stewards.

c. The agenda for the consultation should be set up by the employees who will be involved.

d. Since factual questions can be mastered only by competent understanding, the sort of questions to be discussed should be limited to the ones that pertain directly to the realm of work in which the working group involved in the consultation is engaged. Questions belonging to the realm of managerial responsibility, such as financial, sales, and production policies, do not belong in the work consultation.

It is essential that a consensus be reached among the co-workers in questions relating to new processes of production, new jobs, the flow of work, transportation, delivery of materials, the organization of work, the rate of pay, etc., insofar as these questions fall within the realm of the working group or department.

e. The goal of these consultations is to arrive at a common resolve. If after such a work consultation the superiors are of the opinion that they must decide differently, they must show cause for this to the working group.

f. In order to reach decisions with dispatch, unhampered by bureaucratic red tape, those managers responsible for dealing with the question under discussion should, if it is the will of the working group, be present at the work consultation.

g. There should be room for mutual constructive criticism in the work consultation. Its only legitimate goal is to find the best possible and most tolerable solution for all parties by arriving at a common consensus.

16. Nothing else is being proposed in connection with these work consultations than that from time to time (as a rule, monthly or quarterly), a decision-making process "from the bottom up" be attached to the usual processes of decision-making "from the top down." Indeed, both of these lines will

in fact be dissolved by the mutuality of the convictions reached in the course of the consultation. Those who are "over" and those who are "under" will meet at the same place for common deliberation.

17. It would be a mistake to think that the causes of social conflict in the plant will be completely removed by these consultations. They will not be removed, but, rather, channeled along fruitful lines. In the everyday routine of the plant workers they are always associating with fellow workers of different degrees of authority. Those in charge and those who are led must master their common tasks together. But they view the accomplishment of these tasks from different standpoints. These should be openly expressed and fruitfully compared in work consultations in which every co-worker has the full right to speak.

18. The inclusion of employees as responsible persons in the work process should be initiated on a stepwise and experimental basis, first of all at places that are best suited for such measures. The fact that for more than a century the worker has been rather successfully trained to offer obedient submission at the expense of conscious cooperation, plus the scant experience available with steps moving in the direction indicated above, make it impossible to expect success overnight. But a start has to be made, because: "The chief battle lines in the worldwide struggle of freedom versus servitude run through our plants" (Weinstock).

PART IV. ADDRESSES FOR SOME INDUSTRIAL CELEBRATIONS

10

RADIO ADDRESS:
LABOR DAY, 1960

BREAD, peace, and freedom are the three great watchwords for
the present day in the May manifesto of the International Federation of Free Trade Unions. Bread is obtained by work.
Because work is lacking for millions of men on the face of
the earth, hunger is widespread and movements arise everywhere, from southern Italy to Africa and Asia, to provide work
and thereby bread for mankind. When efforts fail to create
work for all men, peace and freedom may be nice-sounding
slogans, but they help no one. Since the first May Day festival
seventy years ago, work has always been the issue, whether
in the particular form of the question of working hours, or the
demand for work, or the right to strike. Work is the pivotal
point of our industrial development. The date, May 1, has
accumulated a seventy-year history that can be read from the
pages of world history.

One often reads and hears these days that leisure, not work,
is our great problem today. The latter is closely regulated,
stretched across definite periods of time, hedged by precise
instructions, paid for on the basis of exactly calculated production. It seems as if work flows by us like a broad, quiet
river, confined to a safe channel by levees made up of the
laws governing rights, compensation, and codetermination in
work. But leisure time stirs up waves, raging violently back
and forth across the land, rudely overflowing the walls of cus-

tom, morality, decency, and reason. Therefore, one ought to be more concerned with the cultivation of man's leisure-time activities and with his use of the higher wages he has won. Supposedly, that ought to be the main task today for the unions as well as the churches.

We are not of this opinion. For one thing, many more people know how to make meaningful use of their money and leisure time than is generally admitted. Yet it is a fact that money and leisure are problems for the father and mother of a family right up to the present moment. They are problems in an entirely different sense than indicated above, however. How will they obtain both in an appropriate way? Work and leisure are closely connected with each other, since what we undertake *outside* our work depends to a great extent upon what we do *during* our work. If we are merely recipients of orders, who only do what we are told and follow where we are led, we will become accustomed to allowing ourselves to be led in the same way during our leisure time as well. We will passively and willingly submit to the "hidden persuaders" of propaganda and advertisements. It is unfair to raise an outcry about people's lack of willpower and aimlessness if one does not at the same time ask about the roots of this apathy. In our opinion, these are to be found in our present system of work, in the relation of a man to his work and to his fellow workers. Politicians complain about the passive attitude of the people. Union leaders complain about the indifference of millions of workers. No less do the pastors groan about the scarcity of workingmen in their congregations. But precisely in the Evangelical Church, which for over four hundred years has had so much to say about the *ethos* of vocation and work, one ought to know that what happens at a man's place of work is decisive for his whole life. It is unnecessary for us to say anything at this time about the massive changes which the last one hundred and fifty years have brought about in the realm of work. Our point is this: work belongs to man's nature, and he must actualize his nature in his work. If his work becomes a necessary evil for him, a mere appendage to his proper life, a matter of "lost time," then he will lose his humanity.

You will ask wherein the humanity of work consists. Should it perhaps be found in work that is always meaningful, never monotonous, always a joy to do? That would be romanticism. We have to do jobs today that are not always to our liking, that are tedious and hard on the nerves. The weariness of work will remain: if our hands and knees no longer have to tremble under the burden of heavy loads, our nerves will do so all the more. What really has to be changed is the status of those who work in the long chain of production or in providing various sorts of service. Can they be allowed to have a say in their work, to participate in the making of decisions about matters such as *how* their work is organized, evaluated, and rewarded? Can arrangements be found anywhere in the entire world of work that make it possible for the worker and the salaried man, the employer and the official, to speak together with their colleagues or with their employees about *their* work, its preparation, execution, and result? We are not now referring to professional organizations but, rather, to arrangements at the place of work itself that would give those involved there both the right and duty to express their thoughts about the work and to allow these opinions to be openly discussed. Such an arrangement would necessarily break through the insurmountable walls between "the top" and "the bottom," which men on both sides, interestingly enough, continue to speak of in these terms. All the talk about "partnership" and being "co-workers" is an illusion if we do not find forms of work which actualize these fine words. Men do not want merely to be paid for their work. They desire also to be respected as human beings at their place of work. They do not want to be taken as a mere impersonal work force whose efforts are rewarded with pay. Rather, they want to be taken seriously as human beings, as persons who have a desire to think, act, and decide together in their work.

141

Let me repeat: the possibility for such a thing must be provided at the place of work itself. It is not enough simply to direct a man to his leisure time as the realm in which he supposedly may develop his personality because there he is free to decide between a vacation trip to the north or one to the south, or to make whatever other decisions are afforded by the realm in which he is a consumer. To refer him to the political arena for the opportunity of free decision and activity leads to a blind alley, as our daily experiences teach us. The French social observer De Tocqueville saw that 130 years ago during his trip to America: "It is really difficult to see," he said, "how men who have completely renounced the custom of ruling themselves can be in a position to make sound choices of those who are to rule them; and it will not be possible to make anyone believe that a freedom-loving, vigorous, and wise government can ever proceed from the votes of a people of slaves." In another place, De Tocqueville showed that freedom has to be learned, practiced, and proved precisely in the small manageable areas in which a man can make decisions and which he himself can order on the basis of his own abilities.

This area in which a man is technically competent and possesses pertinent knowledge is his place of work, his job. Only when we are able to push aside unfreedom at our place of work will we be able to fill the word "freedom" with real content. For these unfreedoms are the things that make us incapable of taking advantage of freedom on a large scale in order to build a democratic society with it. Listen once more to De Tocqueville: "When it comes to the management of small affairs, for which a sound understanding of human nature is sufficient, they are of the opinion that the citizen is incapable of this; when it comes to the government of the whole nation they entrust the citizen with immense rights; they make out of the citizen, alternately, a plaything and the lord of the sovereign, placing him higher than kings and lower than men." Yes, indeed, the issue is the "management of small affairs," the regulation of our work at the lowest, most manageable level. A man must be able to be active here without fear that his frankness and openness will be rewarded by his being fired by his superior at the earliest opportunity. Going to the polls every four years in national elections or every two years in plant-wide elections is not enough. The worker wants to be asked for his opinions, suggestions, and criticisms concerning his daily work. If one expects of him nothing but simple, unquestioned compliance with and execution of orders, one should not be surprised at a secretly or openly expressed "No." In a case like this, self-respect demands such a response and no one should find fault with it.

What we are talking about is not a matter of the individual man at his place of work, but, rather, of his integration into the group in which he works. The group provides him with the basis upon which his opinions can be validated, and in which he learns to listen to others and to open his mouth, in short, to become "mature." The work group must be the point from which freedom and peace emanate, the seedbed of democracy, the practice field of a social life worthy of man. Such a group and "not the thousandfold individual in the unorganized army of the factory is the unit" (Rosenstock-Huessy) upon which also the representation of a plant might be built up. The discussion of all problems relevant to work belongs in this group. In this way it would become a cell of industrial and social responsibility.

When we hear repeatedly from the ecclesiastical side that Christians have to stand up for human dignity, freedom, and peace, we must not let this end with words. A course of action corresponding to these high goals must be entered upon. We are of the opinion that the way we have outlined above provides us with a chance to crack through old, petrified fronts and to take some practical steps forward toward the realization of human worth, freedom, and peace. Everyone has a chance to attempt a step in this direction, the employer (and he will, most likely, have to be the first to give the green light) and the employee, the officials and everyone else. We believe

143

we may call our fellowmen to move in this direction today in the name of Jesus Christ, who did not want to remain "above," but, rather, came down to us "below" and "lower" among men; who was not bent upon preserving his position of power but exposed himself and his good name to the criticism of all, and does so right up to this very day.

We believe we stand in obedience to this Lord when we attempt to regulate our work in such a way that it can mean bread, freedom, and peace for the whole world.

144

11

AN ADDRESS FOR THE
GRADUATION OF APPRENTICES

WHEN I was asked by the Chamber of Industry and Commerce to give the address at today's ceremony, I considered back and forth what I ought to say. I thought: It mustn't be tiresome. It should pertain to all of them, and even be a help for the times ahead. Whenever a man has such a charge to fulfill, and does not exactly know how he can fulfill it and therefore has some anxiety about it, he ought to take himself to other men, seek their advice and listen to their opinions. Thus, six days in advance, I sat down with workers and other employees, masters and technicians; and then, four days in advance, with apprentices from our Gossner Haus in Kastel; and then, two days ago, I sat down and composed this talk out of what we had discussed. Whether it contains anything right and worthwhile is something each listener will have to decide for himself.

1. One thing was clear from these preparatory discussions: we no longer live in a unified, easily surveyed world, which one might take in all at once as in a panoramic view. On the contrary, it has become extremely complicated. One can hardly construct a picture (*Bild*) of our world any longer, and for this reason there is very little education (*Bildung*) today. Being educated is not merely a matter of knowing and being able to act, but also of the ability to construct a picture of one's

145

world, of the society in which one stands, and of one's own life. For the most part we know only small fragments of these things, and often see nothing beyond the bounds of our own calling and work. But that is a bad situation and leaves us one-sided and stunted. If today we want to shape (*bilden*) our lives, if we desire to become educated (*Gebildete*), or strive to achieve a world picture (*Weltbild*) for our time, then we need other men. There is no work that we can achieve today on our own. Everything calls for *cooperative work*. For this reason, no one may consider the little frog pond in which he swims to be the whole world. Every one of us needs other men in order to be able to fulfill his own work, even the pastor, if he is called on to make a talk like this one.

2. Working together is possible only where men have regard for one another. It is not at all difficult to grasp that the production department needs the sales department, and that the whole process of production is without purpose if the product is not sold, and vice versa. But in practice this insight seems often to be left out of account. Or else why do people speak so badly about each other? Oh, how I myself once and a while work up—I don't know whether it is an unchristian wrath or a holy anger—when I step out of the factory in my worker's clothes and have to go into offices and stores in which I am treated with an air of haughty superiority. Only when they discover that a *Pfarrer* is present do they become civil, and sometimes even excuse themselves. Is our regard for our fellowman so much determined by titles, pocketbooks, and outer garb? Let me see how you carry on with other men, and I will tell you who *you yourself* are! This may soon come to light for many of you who are now thinking of taking out on other apprentices what you yourselves had to bear on your way to becoming journeymen or assistants. Perhaps you will remember the old rule: "Whatsoever you will that others should do to you, do ye to them also." He is a poor wretch who can hold himself above water only by pushing someone else down; who can gain the limelight only by pushing some-

one else into the dark; who must make the others look bad
in order to make himself look good. The way we meet one
another in the pursuit of our callings—the way the man meets
the girl, the salesman the customer, the guest the manager and
vice versa, the salaried man the worker, or the worker the
salaried man, and so on and on—this will show whether we
have regard for our fellowmen. Regard for my fellowman—
be he ever so different from me—is what above all makes me a
man. By disregard for my fellowman I would make myself
inhuman. And who wants to be like that?

3. My friends who helped me in the preparation of this talk
warned me at this point and asked: "Do you really think that
there is so much *freedom* in our vocational life that an individual can really make his own decision?" One has to take so
many things into consideration, and the work itself is often so
narrowly defined and confined that it can be done this way and
only this way. The way is so precisely prescribed that the
individual can move only along the preordained lines. Besides
this, one is always under a pressure from which no one can
escape: What will the others say? "One" does this, "one" buys
that, "one" must wear this, and "one" must conduct himself
so. This little word "one" (*man*) has acquired such power that
it robs us of our freedom even in places where freedom is still
possible. Our way is marked by traffic directions, prohibitory
signs, and prescribed procedures in abundance, to be sure. But
the thing that harasses us most of all is this little word "one."
Perhaps you can remember an hour in which you knew precisely what *you* had to do. But you didn't do it because of
what the others might have said. And then, with a shrug of the
shoulders, you comforted yourselves with the thought: One
must howl with the wolves; you can't swim against the
stream. I know that there are situations in which these maxims
are true. But I doubt that we really must always capitulate to
the wolves. Many times there are muttonheads with whom we
bleat together merely for the sake of simplicity. Yes, it is impossible always to swim against the stream. But I have the

147

impression that we are often dealing not with a stream but with a stinking, stagnant slough, which we stand in only because the others are standing in it. But look, that is something unworthy of man. Nobody ever becomes a free man in this way. We have gotten used to thinking that with a small wager of one mark, thousands can be won. But do you really believe that you can become a genuine man in your life at the risk of only the smallest wager in terms of personal conclusions and decisions? No, humanity is not bought so cheaply. It costs more; for example, it costs the strength *not to do certain things*, but to leave them alone. You know that we are all constantly in danger of being taken as mere consumers. We are everywhere loved if we appear as customers or users. Do we also realize that it takes a lot of energy to protect our personal freedom in many such situations? I feel I have scored a victory, and I feel free, when I have successfully resisted an enticing invitation, e.g., to purchase some kind of commodity or other, such as film. After all are we around merely to go along with, to buy up and consume, whatever someone puts in front of us? Not even a dog does that. He sniffs before he slurps. To be human is to conduct oneself thus: "Test everything and hold onto the good."

Our freedom consists in our ability to choose to do this and not to do that. In the life of our callings certain boundaries are set for us that we cannot step over. But within these limits there is still an area in which we can assert and confirm our freedom. Make use of this in your place of work. Make use of your freedom. Be really free to live as a human being.

4. To be a man means to be a fellowman (*Mitmensch*). This is the last thing I want to say, and, basically, it takes me back to where I began. In the three preceding sections we spoke about the fact that today it is necessary to work together, that this is possible only if we have regard for our fellowmen and do not hold them in contempt, and that we have to make use of our freedom to do this and not to do that in order to fulfill the condition of having regard for our fellowmen. None of you is alone; no one works for himself alone; and

no one is responsible to himself alone. You are men among men; you are fellowmen. Or will one of you say: "The pastor hasn't the slightest notion of how things go with us. Among us there are competitions in which one tries to cut out or overrun the other. Only the ones who know how to use their elbows get ahead. Too much consideration hinders one's promotion"? I believe this is false. In its basic presuppositions, it is completely anachronistic. We can see today in many realms men who once stood over against each other only as enemies now sitting at a table together in conversation, trying to find a common way. Their task is in every case to risk the attempt to see their competitor as a colleague and fellow worker. Colleagues get along much better than competitors. "And what if the other will have none of this?" you may well ask. Then the task is much greater. Then it is a matter of refusing to meet like with like. No, one has to try all the more to understand what you and your colleague are due as men, and thus meet him not as a competitor but as a colleague. It is your responsibility to change the relationship between you and him. You see, in this way your place of work becomes human. Don't expect such bold action—it is really bold—from others. Naturally, "one" doesn't usually do this at all: "one" reacts exactly the way the others act. But you are being "freed" today! Now, make use of this freedom, and become a colleague and fellowman for the others. In this alone is your worth. In the life of your calling a certain *initiative* will be expected of you. Initiative means that you will have to do something for the others before the others address themselves to you. Initiative can be a matter of a friendly look or good word. The most valuable kind of initiative is the kind that is most difficult for you. It will not be something you can calculate in terms of the hour or the right move. But you can be certain that the reward for it will not be withheld. Perhaps it will consist in your being a free man and a genuine human being, both at work and in your free time. More than this, one cannot acquire on earth, and more than this I cannot wish for you on this occasion.

12

A SERMON FOR AN INDUSTRIAL
WORSHIP SERVICE

THE Albert Chemical Works, located at the juncture of the Rhine and the Main rivers, celebrated its one hundredth anniversary on July 11, 1958. The management of the works, after consultation with the Catholic and the Evangelical pastors, scheduled worship services for the respective churches at the beginning of the day's program, which was otherwise completely taken up with a great festival at the Rhine-Main Hall in Wiesbaden, with reception of honored guests, and a Rhine boat excursion for the entire gathering.

Does worship have any legitimate place in such an industrial celebration? Which text should be chosen for such an occasion? Should the entire Sunday liturgy be used? Which hymns seem appropriate? Which prayers? These questions were serious matters not only for the liturgist and the preacher (Horst Krockert and Horst Symanowski), but also for the shift workers of the plant, and even Mr. Albert himself, who discussed these matters for two evenings as their *common* responsibility in the preparation of the worship services.

We cannot here reproduce the entire worship service (i.e., the evangelical service). Therefore we will limit ourselves to the sermon and the concluding prayer.

Sermon Text: Deut. 8:11–20

If today, on the occasion of the one hundredth anniversary of the Albert Chemical Works, we gather early in the morning *in church*, this signifies a confession. We express in this way that we desire God's admonition, perhaps an unpleasant admonition, to confront us. The admonition we are referring to here is the one that was heard long ago from the mouth of Moses, and then perpetuated by the mouths of the Christians, and which today has gone into the whole world. You heard it before, from the altar: "Beware of forgetting him when you can eat to your heart's content, and build fine houses."

It is not a matter to be taken for granted that today none of us really needs to go hungry here, though more than half the human race has to go to bed hungry on this earth, and even now hundreds of thousands of men are starving. Nor is it to be taken for granted that after the severe destruction of the last war and the heavy damage to the plant in 1944, today things have been restored to such an extent that according to the announcement in the festival program, thirty-two million German marks could be invested in the Albert Chemical Works since 1948. Figures like these are hardly comparable to the possessions the Bible speaks about, but the words "Beware that you do not become proud and say of yourself 'My strength and my strong arm have produced this prosperity'" are all the more valid for our time. There are more than enough men who credit to their own account every success that comes their way. But since we are gathered here in God's name and in his presence, we can no longer carry on like that. Rather, we are gathered to hear: "Think much more about the fact that the Lord, your God, who grants you strength, has provided such prosperity."

As I look at some of the familiar faces before me I notice that something is going on at this moment behind their foreheads. They are thinking: Pastor, you talk about prosperity, you repeat the words of the Bible, but you can't really mean

151

us when you talk like this. What you say may well pertain to those in the higher income brackets or to the stockholders, but you cannot mean to include the whole lot of us, as though we were all one lump. And yet I am thinking about all of us, about everyone who lives in this industrial society. We get plenty to eat! Or is there someone among you whose stomach is growling because he didn't have enough to eat for breakfast this morning? We are not without help in cases of sickness, accident, or old age. This, again, is not a self-explanatory matter, since more than one hundred years ago, as the population of Germany and the rest of Europe began to increase at a spectacularly rapid rate, it was by no means to be taken for granted that men had enough to eat. We don't need to look that far back, either, for we know that only ten years ago men worked and still had to go hungry. And we still see this happening today among many people on this earth. But God doesn't want things to be arranged so that some have a lot and the others a little; some to live in super-abundance and others to be in want; some to be satiated or even stuffed while others go hungry.

Certainly there are places in our own land and in our own community where things have to be made a lot better. I am thinking not only of the living conditions under which many of us have to suffer, but also of the inadequate old-age pensions, to cite but two examples. But ever more urgent for us is the question: How will the millions and billions of men today and in the future be adequately fed? Heinrich Albert encountered this question on a smaller scale over one hundred years ago! He saw that Germany's acreage could no longer feed the country's growing population. For this reason, he tried by means of artificial fertilizers to provide the earth with the chemicals it needed. Today it is possible to have enough bread on the table only because the earth is nourished by the products of industry. And this will be even truer in the future. One hundred years ago one could not know the extent to which this would be true. But today we know, and the fact that we do know is significant for all of us, especially those of you who work in a plant like the Albert Chemical Works. You must know that today, precisely through technology and its application in industry, we are to fulfill a command of God: have dominion over the earth!

Did you hear it? It says the *earth, not* man. Have dominion over the *earth!* Make use of the powers of the human spirit, investigate the possibilities of chemistry and physics for allowing a greater number of people to live on earth. Today there are two and eight tenths billion people on the earth. If the population increases at the same rate it has been rising, we will have a population of five billion within forty or fifty years—in other words, double the present population. All of this research, experimentation, production, in short, every bit of work that goes on in industry, does not have its final purpose in profit, in earnings, in personal security, nor even in the existence of a plant such as the Albert Chemical Works. Rather, its sole meaning is in the fact that it *serves man and preserves his life.* You can see this in that one man from Nazareth, who by God's commission was there for men, suffered for them, and died for them. Such a sacrifice for mankind is never asked of us by God. But he expects that we, ignited by this Christ, will also be caught up in his passion for man. If we could converse together at this point, a few skeptical remarks would be forthcoming, and I would be asked whether I have never had any bad experiences with men. When I go into the plant I have a lot of bad experiences, of the kind that men inflict upon each other in the offices as well as in the shops. But if anyone ever had bad experiences with men, it was He who for his goodness was beaten and hung up. Experiences like that go beyond what we have to undergo. And yet he did not resign himself, but refused to give up his passion for men. He stuck to it and persisted in his love for mankind. And that is precisely what he expects from us.

At this point we become somewhat uncertain about the outcome of these past one hundred years, which after all

153

consists not only of buildings and apparatus and ordinances but of men. How many might there have been here in these past one hundred years? Certainly a great number. Were things really conducted for their sakes and for their lives? Are they today? To what end do we live and produce? Why do we bother so much, and why do we know so little about the meaning of our work, namely, that today we are no longer to serve ourselves thereby but to help other men? I know very well how difficult it is today for someone who feels himself a mere number of a cogwheel in a vast factory to understand this and live accordingly. But it is just for this reason that we come together here to allow God to take us by the hand and lead us again in *his* way: "Think much more about the Lord, your God, who grants you strength to achieve such prosperity, *because he wills to keep his covenant* which he swore to your fathers."

Once the rainbow was understood as a sign of God's covenant with man, a sign of the pledge: "I do not desire your ruin, nor the destruction of your life, nor the desolation of the earth." We have Jesus Christ as the seal of this treaty of God with us. He gives us the freedom and the commission to set our work—in laboratories and on the production line, in the offices and among the managers—in the service of our neighbor. Let's say it very clearly: God expects that we in our work, and that the Albert Chemical Works, serve human beings on this earth, and not themselves.

Who doesn't know of the danger of losing sight of this goal, of setting up very different goals in place of this—goals such as personal profits, in small matters as well as large, without consideration of other men, those who are near us and those who are far off? But the Scriptures call this very simply and straightforwardly "idolatry" (*Götzendienst*). But we are not allowed to displace the service of God (*Gottesdienst* = worship)—which includes service of the neighbor—by another kind of service that serves other purposes than man. "If, however, you forget your God, and follow other gods, and serve them and bow before them, then I tell you this day that you will certainly be destroyed." That is the reverse side of God's commission to be there for the sake of other men and to help them get their daily bread and life. That is how serious the message to us is in this worship service, in which we take the opportunity to place this one-hundredth-year celebration *before God*. But the commission and pledge of God is even more encouraging and beautiful, namely, to go to our work, our industrial work, and to serve him and his beloved mankind in this way.

Dear Father in heaven, first of all we must thank you for allowing us to live on this earth. We thank you that you have given man the understanding to win his daily bread from the earth. Thanks be to you that so many men have for a hundred years found work and bread through the Albert Chemical Works.

We ask you to forgive us where self-glorification, pride, and contempt for our fellowmen have taken hold among us. Help us out of our selfishness; enable us to see the man next to us.

Let us not forget those in the world who are hungry. Have mercy upon us that we may not use for our destruction the forces which you have placed into your creation. Permit us to seek and find in this world ways of peace among nations. Permit the Albert Chemical Works to have a place in which, in the future, men will be able to feed themselves and their families through their work; through their dealings with each other prove themselves neighbors; through their products be able to help provide daily bread for others and to silence the hunger of the world. Lord, allow us to live as your children and hear us when we pray as Jesus Christ taught us. "Our Father . . ."

NOTES

1. By Klaus von Bismarck, Haus Villigst, Schwerte/Ruhr.

2. In 1945 most of East Prussia was incorporated into Poland, and the rest into the Soviet Union. The Germans had to leave.

3. Italics mine. The whole Declaration, originally drafted by Karl Barth, constitutes a sharp break both with nineteenth-century liberalism and with traditional Lutheranism; here especially with the latter's interpretation of Luther's doctrine of the two kingdoms. For the full text and a thorough treatment of the history and significance of the Barmen Declaration, see Arthur C. Cochrane, *The Church's Confession Under Hitler* (The Westminster Press, 1962).

4. In *Kirche in der Zeit*, Vol. XVII (January, 1962).

5. Pacifism was almost unheard of in Lutheran Germany prior to 1945. Hence, conscientious objection to military service was not only politically impossible in Hitler's Germany, it was also theologically an almost inconceivable course of action for even the most radical Lutheran opponents of Nazism.

6. Gossner sent 43 missionaries to North America, who worked among the German immigrants on the Midwestern frontier and helped found the Evangelical Synod of North America in 1840, which in 1934 became a part of the Evangelical and Reformed Church, which in turn is now a part of the United Church of Christ. The founder of the society, Johannes Gossner, was also one of the founders of the evangelical movement in Russia (now the Union of Evangelical Christians and Baptists).

7. German theological education does a magnificent job in training ministers to be first-rate Bible scholars and sophisticated theologians, but it devotes very little time to a study of secular society and to the practical task of the church and its ministers.

156

Thus the focus of the ministry tends to be neither the church nor the world—but the minister's study. This in turn tends to lead to a false, introverted theology.

8. For a description of these postwar developments in the German church, see Franklin Littell, *The German Phoenix* (Doubleday & Company, Inc., 1960).

9. *The Evanston Report*, The Second Assembly of the World Council of Churches, 1954 (Harper & Brothers, 1955), p. 106.

10. *Theologische Existenz heute*, new series, No. 45.

11. Cf. Dietrich Bonhoeffer, *Prisoner for God* (The Macmillan Company, 1954), p. 160.

12. Symanowski means his center at Mainz-Kastel, Gossner Haus, mentioned in the Introduction.

13. Since then, weekly celebration of Holy Communion (on Monday morning around the breakfast table, just prior to breakfast), as well as other celebrations of Holy Communion in the evening from time to time, have become regular features of the life of Gossner Haus. Cf. Introduction.

14. *The Evanston Report*, p. 100.

15. *Ibid.*, pp. 104 f.

16. A type of soccer pool based on scores reported in the newspapers of soccer matches all over Europe.

17. Cf. also the concluding reports about Seminar I in *Die Mitarbeit*, 6. Jahrg., Nr. 4; about Seminar II, *ibid.*, 7. Jahrg., Nr. 4; and about Seminar III, *ibid.*, 8. Jahrg., Nr. 5.

18. *Die Mitarbeit*, 6. Jahrg., Nr. 5.

19. H. D. Wendland, *Die Kirche in der modernen Gesellschaft*, 2. Aufl., pp. 127 f.

20. *Ibid.*, p. 183. Insofar as students not studying in the theological faculty are also occasionally allowed to participate in the industrial practicum—since they, too, are members of the church! —they are also taken into the theological discussions of the seminar.

21. Dietrich von Oppen, *Das personale Zeitalter* (Handbücherei des Christen in der Welt, Bd. VII, 1960), p. 9.

22. "While in 1850 fifteen percent of the work energy was provided by men, seventy-nine percent by animals, and six percent by machines, in 1960 the corresponding percentages are three, one, and ninety-six." From: Erich Fromm, *Der moderne Mensch und seine Zukunft* (1960), p. 96.

23. Von Oppen, *op. cit.*, p. 9.

24. "The industrial form of work stands at the center of our entire work life. It has increasingly taken hold of the forms of work in all the other areas in which people are engaged in productive activity and has transformed their inner structure into

its image. As a result, the social problem which arose and developed in the area of industrial work in the nineteenth century has expanded into the other areas of work in the twentieth century and has made them problematical in precisely the same way as happened in industrial work in the previous century." From: Ernst Michel, *Sozialgeschichte der Industriellen Arbeitswelt*, 3. Aufl., p. 9.

25. Cf. on this, Paul Tillich, *The Courage to Be* (Yale University Press, 1959), pp. 116 ff.; and Wolfgang Schweitzer, *Freiheit zum Leben* (Handbücherei des Christen in der Welt, Bd. V, 1959), p. 149.

26. Trutz Rendtorf, "Theologie des Amtes in ihrem Bezug auf die Gesellschaft," in *Die Gemeinde in der modernen Gesellschaft*, Evangelische Akademie Loccum (Hausverlag), p. 38. Rendtorf designates the double requirement referred to above by the not very happy expression "a twofold alienation," which we do not wish to adopt, although we are in agreement with his essential concern.

27. Cf. Von Oppen, *op. cit.*, p. 50.

28. *Die Mitarbeit*, 8. Jahrg., Nr. 5.

29. "When we speak in abbreviated fashion of 'society,' we have in mind the concrete social body which has developed historically into a relative unity, which has expressed this unity in a political order and form, and which has at the same time entered the stage of technologized, pluralistic, industrial social order." From: H. D. Wendland, "Gesellschaftliche Diakonie," in "Aufgabe der gesellschaftlichen Diakonie," *Kirche im Volk*, Heft 25 (1960), p. 41.

30. Von Oppen, *op. cit.*, p. 50.

31. Cf. for this, *The Evanston Report*, which confirmed this introversion in all the churches throughout the world.

32. H. D. Wendland, *Die Kirche in der modernen Gesellschaft*, p. 250.

33. Eugen Rosenstock-Huessy, *Heilkraft und Wahrheit* (1952), p. 24.

34. Dietrich Bonhoeffer, *Ethics* (The Macmillan Company, 1955), p. 60.

35. Cf. the very useful little writing of Jürgen Moltmann, *Die Gemeinde im Horizont der Herrschaft Christi* (1959).

36. "Accepting acceptance through being unacceptable is the basis for the courage of confidence." (Paul Tillich, *op. cit.*, pp. 164 f.)

37. Cf. Von Oppen, *op. cit.*, pp. 212 ff., and also the liberating lecture of the same author, "Strukturfragen der christlichen Gemeinde in der mobilen Welt," printed in the collection of lectures at Loccum referred to in note 26, above.

38. R. Bohren, "Unsere Kausalpraxis—eine missionarische Ange-legenheit?" *Theologische Existenz heute,* new series, No. 83, p. 11.

39. Among others: T. Rendtorf, *Die soziale Struktur der Gemeinde* (1958); H. O. Wölber, *Religion ohne Entscheidung* (1959); R. Köster, *Die Kirchentreuen* (1959).

40. On the question of "The *Diakonia* of the Church in the Industrial World," see the essay by Robert Starbuck under the same title in "Aufgabe der gesellschaftlichen Diakonie," *Kirche im Volk,* Heft 25, pp. 48 ff. A shorter English version of the same essay may be found under the title "Industrial Evangelism Today," in *History's Lessons for Tomorrow's Mission* (World's Student Christian Federation, Geneva, 1960), pp. 232 ff.

41. Cf. the discussion of the author in his address at the Munich *Kirchentag* in 1959, "Church Without Walls"; originally printed in "Gegen die Weltfremdheit," *Theologische Existenz heute,* new series, No. 79.

42. J. Matthes, "Die volkskirchliche Gemeinde im Sicht des Soziologen," in the collection of Loccum lectures referred to in note 26, pp. 151 f.

43. *Ibid.,* p. 153.

44. H. D. Wendland, *Die Kirche in der modernen Gesellschaft,* p. 253: "Without experiments, no experience, no investigation of the real world. This applies to the action of the church, too. . . . We cannot act and preach as the church without thinking theo-logically, but we will not be thinking theologically without risking action and speaking."

45. The significance of this triad for the renewal of the church cannot be explored any further in this report. The Dutch theo-logian Hoekendijk has sharpened the definition of this triad: *kērygma* = proclamation of salvation; *diakonia* = demonstration of salvation; *koinōnia* = participation in salvation. Cf. also R. Star-buck, *loc. cit.,* and R. Bohren, *loc. cit.,* who have taken over this ecclesiological triad.

46. The penetrating basis for this transformation may be found in Hendrik Kraemer, *A Theology of the Laity* (The Westminster Press, 1958). Cf. also Hans-Ruedi Weber, "Mündige Gemeinde," in *The Ecumenical Review,* Vol. I (1960); and G. Webber, *God's Colony in Man's World* (Abingdon Press, 1960), p. 129, where the work of the East Harlem Protestant Parish in New York is described: "The real task of the colony is outside its walls in the world. The work of the colonists is where they spend their lives. . . . The minister . . . is to prepare the colonists for their work and ministry in the world. . . . The minister, that is to say, the ordained clergyman, exists in the Church for the sake of the world,

and the laity exists in the world for the sake of the Church."
On this point, see especially Markus Barth, *The Broken Wall*
(American Baptist Publication Society, 1961).

47. Often described by the author, most recently in *Theologische
Existenz heute*, new series, No. 79, and in Langhans, "Gemeinde
—veranstaltungen . . ." (1961).

48. A similar Eucharistic practice may be found in the house
church movement in Leeds, England. Cf. Ernest W. Southcott,
The Parish Comes Alive (Morehouse-Gorham Co., 1956).

49. Where, as in the previously mentioned house church movement in Leeds, the Lord's Supper has been taken into homes, not
only the family proper but an entire *oikos* fellowship gathers after
the New Testament pattern. Friends, co-workers, their families,
godparents, and godchildren are all involved.

50. Cf. H. D. Wendland, in *Kirche im Volk*, Heft 25, pp. 44 f.

51. Johannes Doehring, "Das Leben in der 'offenen Gemeinde,' "
in *Die Gemeinde in der modernen Gesellschaft*, p. 137. Doehring
continues at the place cited: "That kind of apostolate must recede
into the background which, like a bridge whose span becomes
usable only because of the strength derived from the supporting
pillars, has to rest on the support of the pastoral office. Otherwise
the church, with its fifteen thousand sermons every Sunday in
Germany alone, will look like so many of the bridges that were
blasted during the last war. The pillars remained standing. But no
one could cross the chasm between them anymore."

52. A play on the Latin root, *pati*, which means "to suffer," or
"to endure."

53. Children of working parents who carry their house key on
a string around their necks.

54. Martin Luther, *The Right and Power of a Christian Congre-
gation to Judge All Teaching, and to Call, Appoint, and Dismiss
Teachers, Established and Proved from Scripture*, in *Works of
Martin Luther*, Vol. IV (Philadelphia Edition, 1915–1932).

55. *Ibid.*, p. 79. We prefer to render the last two words, "*zum
Priester*," "to be a priest," instead of the Philadelphia edition's,
"to the priesthood."

56. Luther, *op. cit.*

57. German pastors usually begin their sermons with the salu-
tation *Liebe Gemeinde*.

58. The last Monday before Lent.

59. Cf. Mark 10:36, 51. (Translator's note.)

60. Full-time lay church workers who have received special
training (a one-year course) at the *Evangelische Sozialakademie*
in Friedewald.

160